HOLY

Holy Fire

JOHN FERGUSSON

KINGSWAY PUBLICATIONS
EASTBOURNE

ISBN 0 85476 626 X

Designed and produced by
Bookprint Creative Services
P.O. Box 827, BN21 3YJ, England for
KINGSWAY PUBLICATIONS LTD
Lottbridge Drove, Eastbourne, E. Sussex BN23 6NT.
Printed in Great Britain.

This book is dedicated to my brother
Robert Fergusson
without whose persistent prayers
I may never have known Christ.

Acknowledgements

I praise God from whom all inspiration flows.

No book is the labour of just one man. First of all I want to thank Reinhard Bonnke, not just for writing the Foreword, and for giving me unrivalled opportunity to minister the good news of Jesus Christ around the world, but also for sparing me from my duties for long enough to find the time to write this book.

I wish to thank Alan Vincent for invaluable advice and comment, Rob Birkbeck for technical assistance with production; Rachael and James Birkbeck for the original idea on which the cover was based; and my wife Bron for proof-reading the whole text, word by word. If any mistakes remain, it was I who made those. They made the corrections that you don't see!

John B. Fergusson

Contents

Foreword

John Fergusson is a Crusade Director of Christ for all
Nations and has, together with his wife Bron, success-
fully prepared numerous gospel crusades in different
parts of the world. I have come not just to appreciate
John's organisational skills, but also his spiritual zeal as
a man of God. He is a minister of the gospel in his own
right, and his Bible studies have thrilled and blessed many
churches in many countries.

Holy Fire is his first book, and I heartily recommend it.
It is a treasure trove for those who want to understand the
fire of the Holy Spirit and move in its glorious power.
John is very sensitive to the promptings of the Spirit of
God, he flows with the gifts, and has been used propheti-
cally in remarkable ways. When reading this book, one
comes to the bottom of it. *Holy Fire* will inspire Christians
to trust God for this glory-heat in their own lives and
ministries.

Reinhard Bonnke
July 1995

Introduction

Fire is fascinating. Used by man from the beginning of time, fire has been an integral part of his culture, his livelihood, his destiny. It has always intrigued us, and yet we have never fully comprehended it. Everyone knows the mesmeric quality of an open flame, but can anyone explain why we should find it so inherently attractive? What is it about the very nature of it that draws us, enthrals us, beguiles us? Why should something so quintessentially destructive seem almost to enchant us? Is it some kind of subliminal death-wish?

Fire is a key biblical theme, its imagery is powerful. Fire destroys, cleanses, separates, enlightens, empowers, motivates, tests, refines, consumes, endangers, burns. All these lessons are taught us through the medium and means of fire in the Scriptures, and yet there is something much more—much deeper—like a hidden river flowing beneath the surface of the revelations of God's word, every now and then springing to the surface to reveal itself in power, and then disappearing again from our gaze. But all along we are aware of its presence, its subterranean power, ready at any moment suddenly to appear once more. This pattern in Scripture is reflected throughout the history of revival, and is especially relevant today as the worldwide church is experiencing another outpouring of fire. Why now? Why today?

13

There almost seems to be an inconsistency, a randomness to the appearance of God's fire throughout the Bible. On many occasions we wonder why God uses it at all. Why the burning bush? Why Sodom and Gomorrah (and why not Babylon?)? Why the fiery furnace; the fire on Mount Carmel; the lake of burning sulphur? What is it about the nature of fire that is so important? Is there a common thread? What does God tell us of his own nature, his own character, through this strange, compulsive, captivating, destructive, fundamental element of God's creation?

And how can this short study aid us in the service of our Lord? I do not set out merely to titillate our desire to learn for the sake of diversion, like the men of the Areopagus in Acts 17, even though it is God's word we study. My heart is that we better furnish ourselves for the task that God has set us, by a deeper understanding of his character, his command, his call and his equipping.

First, it concerns me deeply that the church today, in large part, lacks a true sense of the awesomeness of God. The original church certainly knew what it was to fear the Lord, not least through such dramatic manifestations of God as the deaths of Ananias and Sapphira.

Many of our traditional denominations, while historically teaching the fear and reverence of the Lord, now sadly reserve much of that reverence for the rituals and traditions established for the purpose of deflecting just such errors. In more recent renewals the consequent backlash has inevitably emphasised the joy and spiritual experience of salvation and fullness or baptism of the Holy Spirit, and some have not only lost an understanding of the meaning of the 'fear of Jacob', but, at the extreme, worship has degenerated into irreverent self-gratification, albeit with spiritual meat.

At the end of Ecclesiastes we are exhorted to: 'Fear God and keep his commandments, for this is the whole duty of man. For God will bring every deed into judgment, including every hidden thing, whether it is good or evil' (Eccles 12:13–14). It is my sincere desire that some of what we discover here will bring a renewed sense of the nature of the holiness of God. Though he urges us to call him 'Abba', our heavenly Father is no sugar-daddy. His name is also 'Jealous'. The fire of God is Holy Fire.

Throughout history, every revival has brought tremendous blessing and great fruit, but the concern of many has been that they seem inevitably to be accompanied by excess, prompted by human nature ('emotionalism'), which proves to be the fly in the ointment which makes the anointing stink. It is my prayer that this book will bring a balance through a better understanding of the essentially *holy* nature of this fire. The Holy Spirit is to be enjoyed, yes. But he is not a plaything. Fire is beautiful, but hot!

In this sense this book is a cautionary tale—I am reminded of the doggerel I learned as a child:

> Boy with pliers
> Electric wires
> Blue flashes
> Boy ashes

My second purpose is to bring to light some of the astonishing manifestations of the love of God. As we begin to appreciate the severity of crossing God's boundaries, so we can understand better his eternal loving-kindness towards his own mankind, as he gracefully allows error after error, deliberate or otherwise, and his mighty provision for his beloved people in the sacrifice of our Lord and Saviour, Jesus Christ. To comprehend better the awesome power of his holiness is to appreciate more deeply the supreme compassion of the gospel message.

Some of the conclusions here are surprising perhaps. I

do not wish to be a 'revealer of new truths', but merely to set out what Scripture has been saying to me, powerfully and urgently, that others may be encouraged and enlarged.

I first stumbled upon many of the basic concepts shared here during the preparation of a crusade for Reinhard Bonnke in Buenos Aires, Argentina, in 1992. The diverse duties of a crusade director include visiting churches, stirring up the congregations to become involved in the campaign. Thousands of workers are needed, and we try to mobilise as great an army as possible. We had decided to call the Argentine event '*Cruzada de Fuego*' which means 'Fire Crusade', and I had been asked by the committee to speak in a series of promotional meetings around the city.

The subject of the fire of God seemed to choose itself, and I set to studying the Scriptures with zest. New revelation followed new revelation as the Holy Spirit spoke to me from the pages, and I was astounded by what he showed me. Never had I heard such things said or preached. The more I read, the more I saw; and the more I preached it, the more it grew in my mouth. I found myself preaching things from the pulpit which I had never known until that very moment. It was as though there was a hotline direct from heaven. The messages carried an anointing which I had never experienced before, and they still carry it today, whenever I share these same truths.

For me, as a relative beginner in these things, it was without doubt the most exciting thing that had ever happened to me, and I soon realised that I would have to start writing it all down. Again, as I have done so, more and more understanding has come, as has the urgency to share what I believe is a vital message for today's church. It is this fire shut up in my bones that like Jeremiah I cannot hold in. Here it is. I am delivered of it!

Finally, where through these pages God has clarified

some half-buried truth to you, then I give him all the praise and glory. And where through my own muddled thinking I stray from the genuine truth of his word, I beg your forgiveness, and pray that nothing of my own thoughts will find a permanent resting place in your mind, but only what the Holy Spirit might emphasise to you. Please seek his guidance to give you the discernment that I lack in such cases.

1

Divine Deliverances

Three young men

Azariah and his friends Hananiah and Mishael were no
ordinary men. They were young, in their prime—tall,
strong, muscular, good-looking. They were the *crème de
la crème* of the noble families of Judah.

Not only that, they had undergone and passed stringent
tests and exams for general knowledge, aptitude and
intelligence. They were clever, sharp as the swords they
could so deftly handle and quick to learn. They had been
selected from among many to undergo three years of
intensive training in language and literature, and were to
be given the best food in the land to aid them in their
studies. After completing these, they were to enter the
king's service. They were top scholarship material.

They were also devoted to God, and due to their
unbending allegiance to him, God added to the lessons
of their teachers, giving them a godly understanding of
learning and literature, so that when the king himself
finally questioned them, there was no one to match them
in wisdom and understanding, which surpassed by ten
times that of the established authorities of the day. Truly
God had brought these three to the heights of human
achievement. Was anyone ever so well qualified, so well
trained? Today we marvel at the prowess of our athletes,

but I suspect they would pale into insignificance in the face of these almost superhuman three.

But the greatest test of their lives was still to come, and it would not test their learning, but their hearts.

The great challenges of this life involve a battle of the mind before the battle on the ground. First must come the mental victory. Mary had said, 'Let it be to me as you have said,' to the angel Gabriel, long before she had to cope with the dragging months of a pregnancy outside of marriage, with all that that implied. But she already had the victory, which enabled her to overcome the emotional struggle.

Jesus himself, in the Garden of Gethsemane, had prayed on his knees before the Father, 'Yet not my will, but yours be done.' That was the great test, not later on the cross, which was merely an acting out of the victory already won. Each of us faces the same crisis of our faith every time we are tested, and when we have *that* victory, the physical victory follows as surely as dawn follows night.

So it was for Shadrach, Meshach and Abednego, for such were the Babylonian names of our three heroes. All their great learning and education, all their great wisdom—even though God himself had endorsed and strengthened these very things in his children—all were of small account to the Lord, the great tester of hearts.

Already they had demonstrated their loyalty to his name when they insisted that God could feed them better than the king could, and so it had proved. They had proved faithful in small things. But God had a greater plan, and would need a more powerful demonstration of their loyalty, so that his miracle-working power might be made manifest. For God had in mind not merely the salvation of three men, but the complete deliverance of his people from the dangers of the bondage they faced daily.

So finally the great day came. Daniel 3 gives the full

account. Shadrach and the others, by now chief adminis-
trators through the intervention of their friend Daniel,
were faced with a royal edict to worship the astonishing
statue of Nebuchadnezzar himself—27 metres high, and
made of gold. The sycophants bowed and scraped, but the
three refused. Their courage was impressive, but perhaps
they did not fully understand the consequences. But when
they came before the king, and saw all the high officials,
the musicians, the crowds, the festivities—and the furnace—they knew. Now came the great test; their Garden
of Gethsemane. How easy it would have been to go along
with the request of the king. Were they not some of the
highest men in the land? Would their position of such
influence not give them years of opportunity to testify
about their God to the courts of power? But they knew
their God, and they knew their Scripture. And their reply
to the command of the king revealed the same audacity
and the same understanding as Jesus before Pilate: 'O
Nebuchadnezzar, we do not need to defend ourselves
before you in this matter.' What a statement! What
victory! Now the battle was already won. What happened
on the ground would now be fulfilled. God could (and
would!) deliver.

Respectfully, they were saying, 'You are not our
judge—there is a higher authority and our case rests
before him. Your decisions are unimportant. We are
only here because God wants us to be here, and we trust
him rather than you. Our lives are in his hands, not yours.
If he wanted, he could send an army of angels and deliver
us at this very moment.' Perhaps they had expected that
very thing to happen. Were they already looking around
them, waiting, hoping? No, they knew that God was able
even to deliver them from the furnace. In the face of such
an impossible situation, they trusted God. Abraham had
said to Isaac, 'God will provide the sacrifice.' Who knows

exactly what he had in mind, but God *did* provide it, and so he always will.

But what was in their minds as they were tied up by the strongest of Nebuchadnezzar's soldiers? They knew they had made the right decision, but where was the deliverance? Or did God really want them to die? How could all those years of preparation be reduced to a few ounces of ashes? Had they been trained, honed, perfected to be so glibly discarded?

The stokers worked furiously. The bellows belched air into the roaring flames. The searing heat could be almost grasped. The crowd fell silent as the king shouted in his anger, '*Throw them in!*' The soldiers grabbed them, bound them tightly and ran towards the white-hot furnace, shielding their faces from the intensity of the fire.

A supernatural climax

At this point of high emergency, we must pause. For there seems to be an incongruity. I puzzled over it for years, until I suddenly saw the truth. Truth which has opened up such a wonderful treasure chest of revelation that I have felt compelled to share it. For the Bible says: 'The flames of the fire killed the soldiers who took up Shadrach, Meshach and Abednego' (Dan 3:22).

But, however hot the fire, and however urgent the command of the king, I cannot believe that the soldiers could run close enough to the fire by their own will to kill themselves. Obey orders, yes, but they were not bent on suicide. When Shadrach, Meshach and Abednego were thrown into the furnace, *something happened*. Something supernatural.

We know from the story that the three victims were not killed. That in itself is miracle enough for the story to have passed down to us through these pages. But the soldiers *were* killed, instantly. That miracle has been overlooked. But it tells us a great truth.

I believe what happened is this—at the moment when the three were thrown into the fire, there was a great heat flash! Now, the furnace was seven times hotter than normal, as hot as the technology of the day knew how. Man couldn't have made it hotter. Therefore that heat flash was from God. It was Holy Fire! Far hotter than man could make and far more potent. And the soldiers, already as close as they could get, and probably already getting burned, were instantly consumed by the holy flash of heat.

And suddenly the three were walking around in the fire, with a fourth who looked 'like a son of the gods', according to the description of the king. And it says in the same verse (3:25) that they were unbound and unharmed. How amazing! The normal effect of the furnace would have been to consume them in a matter of seconds. They should have died instantly, burst into flames, and been reduced to cinders in less time than it takes to read this sentence. But they were no longer in a normal furnace! They were in the furnace of the Holy Fire of God, and that, as we shall see, is altogether different.

· Let us look at the effect of this Holy Fire on our three friends (for we already know the effect on the soldiers!), and we will begin to learn something of the nature of this Holy Fire.

The nature of Holy Fire

First, they were unbound and unharmed. They had been thrown in tightly bound, complete with their full clothes, including turbans, which we read later were totally unsinged, and now their bindings had fallen off, or burned up. Either way, they had disappeared so that they were now totally free. So our first lesson is that the Holy Fire of God liberates and sets free! 'So if the Son sets you free, you will be free indeed' (Jn 8:36).

When the fire of God falls, there is freedom for the captives. All the bonds of Satan fall off. However tightly we are bound, the Holy Fire destroys the bindings and releases us. And in the worst possible situation imaginable, bound tight in that furnace, the Holy Fire delivered. Surely nothing, not even the fiercest fiery furnace, can separate us from the love of God. *God's Holy Fire is a liberating fire.*

And not only were they free, but unharmed! So the Holy Fire did not destroy a single thread of their clothing, nor a hair on their head. For it says that there was no smell of fire upon them. Nothing was burned. Nothing was harmed. Nothing was destroyed. 'When you walk through the fire, you will not be burned; the flames will not set you ablaze' (Is 43:2). And yet the bonds which held them, which had been tied by the soldiers, and which did not belong to them, were totally and instantly destroyed. *God's Holy Fire is a protective fire.*

Thirdly, they were walking around in full view of the king and the crowd. They weren't just sitting down enjoying the heat. They were active, and in total control of the situation, demonstrating for all the world to see that they were untouched by this evil furnace. God's Holy Fire stimulates to action, not to lethargy, and when it comes, the world knows. The Holy Fire of God brings a demonstration of his active power. This same active power had killed the soldiers. *God's Holy Fire is powerful.*

Never mind if they had been looking for angels earlier. It did not matter. But I am sure they didn't expect to meet one right in the fire! It is often considered that this one who looked like a 'son of the gods' was actually the Son of God himself. If so, then within the Holy Fire of God there is a divine presence. So, fourthly, therefore, they were not alone. *God's Holy Fire brings the presence of God.*

So to the three, God's chosen, the Holy Fire brought freedom, protection, motivation and power, and his divine presence. It brought another thing too. Before the ordeal of the furnace, they were being persecuted and plotted against. Afterwards, the king himself recognised them as 'servants of the Most High God', and promptly promoted them (v. 30). Recognition may therefore be added to the list. God brings glory to his servants as they learn to obey him. Victory over their enemies is 'the glory of all his saints' (Ps 149:9).

Of course Shadrach, Meshach and Abednego were not the only ones affected by the Holy Fire. King Nebuchadnezzar himself was not only astonished, but converted! He gives praise and glory to God, declaring that 'no other god can save in this way'. His whole attitude to God changed. Here was someone who was the very epitome of an unbeliever—the king of pagan Babylon no less—whose whole life was changed by a demonstration of the Holy Fire of God in action. How relevant this is to us today shall be clearly revealed in later chapters.

For now, let us find another demonstration of Holy Fire and see if it confirms our findings from this story.

A pillar of fire

Turn the pages back to the shores of the Red Sea, and another slavery. A choking dust cloud hangs over a vast movement of people, the air sibilant with a multitude of voices, of distant cries, coughing goats, creaking carts, urgent tramping feet. A seething swell of humanity presses on through the heat and the flies. Driving them on is the fear of the fugitive, mingled with the desperate hope of freedom.

Astonishingly, however, a darker, vertical pillar is clearly visible ahead of the throng among the dust. For the Israelites are leaving Egypt, and the Lord is leading them out. Before they even came to the Red Sea the cloud had appeared before them, and even more amazingly, it had seemed like a pillar of fire at night. Despite their apprehension of such a phenomenon, their fear of the Egyptians was the greater, urging them on into the desert. Was this really the Lord guiding them, as Moses would have them believe?

And now with their backs to the water, they watched the approaching army of Pharaoh with utter dread, certain of their destruction at last. But suddenly someone notices that the pillar of cloud which they had stopped watching some while ago had shifted. Now it was moving between them and the Egyptians. Surely God couldn't mean them to follow it back into the teeth of certain death? At that moment, a great swell of movement behind them caused them to turn and see the impossible. With astonished eyes, they watched as thousands of their fellow Israelites began to rush straight into the sea. And with greater astonishment still, they now saw the sea itself rising up like two great cliffs, as if held back by vast walls of glass. A strange light shone from the glowing pillar of fire upon the whole great mass of people, clearly lighting up their way. Without another backward glance and with all possible speed they pressed on, down between the towering, impossible walls of water, straining every muscle to get through, and every nerve to watch the sea.

But where was the pursuing army? The pillar of fire seemed to shine only in the direction of the fleeing Israelites. Behind the cloud all was as dark as pitch, and nothing could be seen of Pharaoh and his men. And all the time the press struggled forward through the long, long night, the chill air echoing with shouts and cries ringing through the chasm in the sea.

As the first light of dawn coloured the sky ahead, the last of the stragglers of the vast throng struggled up the far side of the seashore and turned to see the Egyptians following through the sea. But their momentary fear gave way to relief as they saw the total confusion behind them.

Soldiers were milling around broken chariots, commanders were vainly gyrating their arms to hordes of slaves who were impotently trying to hoist the crippled vehicles out of the way of the impatient soldiers; horsemen struggled to stay mounted as their horses shied and whinnied at the din. Then, as they watched, those in the front began to turn and head back into the sea! Suddenly a panic seemed to strike the soldiers as the whole army desperately attempted to escape another mighty plague of this awesome God. The surge of terrified Egyptians poured blindly back through the chasm of water. And with a roar such as the watchers had never before heard, the liquid cliffs let go and drove together with the force of an earthquake. A vast wave ricocheted down the sea, and bits of debris could be seen in the swirling mass of water—all that was left of Pharaoh's legions. Such was the miracle.

But what of the fire of God? The Bible tells us quite a lot about this pillar of fire and pillar of cloud. In Exodus 13:21 it says: 'The Lord went ahead of them in a pillar of cloud. . . .' So, first, the Lord *inhabited* the pillar. Just like the fourth man in the furnace in the book of Daniel, the Lord was there.

Secondly, the pillar was God's chosen method of leading his people to freedom. The story of the crossing of the Red Sea has epitomised freedom for thousands of years.

By a miracle too audacious for any novelist to have dared invent, God led his enslaved people to freedom. The parallels with our salvation in Jesus Christ are legion and legendary. Here is freedom by God's mighty hand, and the leading is by the fire of God!

Thirdly, God does an amazing thing with this pillar. During the crossing of the sea, when the crisis was at its height and when the Egyptians would surely have caught up with the multitude, the pillar moves *behind* the Israelites, lighting their own path, but obscuring that of the pursuers. God's Holy Fire, for that is surely what this pillar is, is a protecting fire, providing light to God's people, but darkness to their enemies. Just as the appearance of the Holy Fire in the furnace protected the three men of God, so here it moves to protect the whole of God's people. And God protects actively, not passively. He moved actively to protect his people. That he should do it through provision of light to those protected and of darkness to the aggressors is not only full of symbolism, but so true to the whole character of God himself. 'For the message of the cross is foolishness to those who are perishing, but to us who are being saved it is the power of God' (1 Cor 1:18).

That protection culminated in the ultimate destruction of the enemies and enslavers of God's people, as his protection does today through the blood of Jesus, which as we read in Revelation 12:11 is an essential ingredient in the overcoming of Satan.

Just as Shadrach, Meshach and Abednego didn't just sit down in the fire but walked around, so here the Israelites were not lifted bodily to the other side of the sea, as God could just as easily have accomplished, but were simply given two miraculous provisions: that of the open sea and that of the light to travel through it; and they were expected to get on and make something of these provisions. God worked the miracles, but the Israelites had to work at their escape. So not only did God provide protection, but motivation for action. As Reinhard Bonnke has said, there is no such thing as an anointed couch potato. Or as the 'old wives' have it: 'God helps those who help themselves.' This does not mean, and has never meant, that salvation is a matter of picking ourselves up by our bootstraps. Indeed that is the root error of all false religions. God provides *his* solution for our salvation, expecting, even requiring, us to lay hold of his provision by faith.

And it took faith for every single one of the whole enormous, jostling, shoving, sweating, exhausted crowd to step between those walls of water—faith that their God who delivers, who protects and who provides through his mighty miraculous power, would not now allow them to perish, but see them to safety on the other side.

Also, we saw that when the Holy Fire of God fell into the furnace, God's chosen people who stepped out of it were at once accorded honour and recognition that they were his. Just so the Israelites from the sea. Interestingly, in Moses' famous prayer of intercession for Israel in Numbers 14, he uses this very recognition as a key argument against God's planned destruction of such a wayward and rebellious nation: 'The inhabitants of this land . . . have already heard [cries Moses] that you . . . go before them in a pillar of cloud by day and a pillar of fire by night' (Num 14:14). 'The world already knows that they are your people,' he is saying in effect, 'and that if you destroy them now, it will not glorify your name.'

God goes so far to be associated with his own people that it seems he cannot escape from being involved in their destiny, however sinful they become. He is trapped by his own love. The ultimate truth of this he demonstrates on the cross, being unwilling to escape even the final destiny of man, which is to die.

What happened to the Egyptians—the ones whom God was determined should know exactly who he was through this divine intervention of his Holy Fire? In verse 24 of Exodus 14 we read: 'During the last watch of the night the Lord looked down from the pillar of fire and cloud at the Egyptian army and threw it into confusion.' And then, just like the soldiers in the first story we studied, they were completely destroyed, unable to exist when confronted with the Holy Fire of the living God. So, once again, the Holy Fire of God is discriminating against some and favouring others.

So all the same characteristics of Holy Fire are here too—freedom, protection, motivation to action, his divine presence, recognition (or, perhaps better, identification) and discriminatory power. There is of course a seventh, and that is his guidance. In this episode, we read that the prime purpose of the pillar was to guide God's people 'so that they could travel by day or night' (Exod 13:21).

Shadrach and the others didn't need much guidance in the fiery furnace, so there was no need for this provision. Here, however, the Israelites' prime need was a guide, to lead them through the alien and unknown desert.

Not only was that need accommodated, but consistently with God's character (for consistency *is* God's character), we read that the pillar never left them: 'Neither the pillar of cloud by day nor the pillar of fire by night left its place in front of the people' (Exod 13:22). It was there day in day out, and night in night out, during all their travels. Presumably it did not leave them until they no longer had need of it, when they entered the Promised Land. This fire of guidance, then, is our assurance of direction until we too no longer have need of it; that is, when we have finally arrived to be with God in his glory. Meanwhile, the cloud is there by day and the fire by night to 'search out places for you to camp and to show you the way you should go' (Deut 1:33). When to stop, and for how long; when to travel and where.

In fact the whole law of God, our ultimate written guide from God, came to us out of the fire on Mount Sinai. The Ten Commandments are prefaced with, 'The Lord spoke to you face to face out of the fire on the mountain' (Deut 5:4). The fire brought forth the law.

In these miraculous manifestations of the Holy Fire of God, we learn something of its character. Many of these characteristics are hauntingly familiar. Where have we seen them before? And another thing. We have seen that the Holy Fire has markedly different effects on different people. Why? What is happening? To find the answer, let us look at another manifestation: the burning bush.

2

A Consuming Fire

The holy bush

The similarities between this and the first of the two previous stories is remarkable.

First, like the three heroes of the previous chapter, Moses was one of God's chosen people. From birth, in fact, he had been recognised as a special child, and the protection of God had covered him miraculously. Again, he had been educated with all the best wisdom and knowledge of the day.

In this very incident, the story of the burning bush, God called Moses, by name, to his great life work, even though he was eighty years old. Even though he had 'backslidden' in the desert for forty years, God at last confronted him. It seems highly probable that Moses himself was finally seeking God. Why else did he go to the trouble of taking the flock 'to the far side of the desert' (Exod 3:1) and specifically to 'the mountain of God' as we are told? I sometimes wonder how long God had been trying to appear to Moses, in whatever form, but Moses hadn't been paying any attention. But now, perhaps, he had decided that eighty years was a good enough innings, and that he should make his peace with God before his final departure. Whatever Moses' motives or expectations were as he journeyed, God (as is so often the case) had different plans.

Secondly, this confrontation with the Lord totally changed Moses' life, just as it had changed those of Shadrach, Meshach and Abednego, and even King Nebuchadnezzar.

And here too we have a fire. Why should God appear in such a strange way? Why choose to appear in flames in a bush? Because God wanted not only to speak, but to demonstrate. Notice that what was in the fire, in this case the bush, was not consumed—in fact it was protected, just as Shadrach, Meshach and Abednego were. Even Moses was not allowed to approach it. Secondly, God spoke from the bush, so we have divine presence. Thirdly, Moses was liberated from the forty years of desert living and was returned to his people in the power and authority of God. Freedom. And finally, God demonstrated his divine active power in signs and wonders, which even Moses himself was enabled to perform, and which would give him recognition among his people. So we already have signs of Holy Fire that we saw in the previous chapter: presence, power, protection, recognition and freedom.

Now let us see how God addresses Moses from the bush. First, he calls him by name. But then he tells Moses to take off his sandals, because he is standing on holy ground. I have often puzzled over this. How come this remote spot at the back of the desert on the mountain of God was holy? What was so special about that particular spot? And suddenly I realised what was happening. Actually the spot itself was not important. It could have happened anywhere in the desert, or out of it for that matter. God is showing us *why* the bush was not burned . . . because the ground on which it was standing, and therefore the bush itself, had been pronounced holy by

God himself, so that the bush would not be burned. Here is the great truth. *The bush did not burn, because it was holy!*

For the purposes of this meeting, God wanted to attract Moses' attention (and teach us all a lesson into the bargain), and he did this through appearing via his angel in flames of Holy Fire. And in order that the bush should not be consumed, God proclaimed it holy.

Now let us check back with Shadrach, Meshach and Abednego, whom we left walking around in the fiery furnace. Now we see that the reason they were unharmed by the Holy Fire of God, was because God deemed them to be holy. God proclaims that 'the righteous shall live by faith', and these three had declared *by faith*: 'The God we serve is able to save us from it, and he will rescue us from your hand, O king' (Dan 3:17). By that faith, God deemed them righteous.

Conversely, that is why the soldiers were instantly consumed—they were not holy. Wow! The more I think about that the more awed I am. We find ourselves face to face with all the universe-creating power of God. Suddenly, like Adam, I feel very small and very naked.

Of course the Egyptians suffered a similar fate for similar reasons. The unholy enemies of God's people thought that they could overtake the holy, but they reckoned without the Holy Fire. Their fate was sealed the moment Moses prophesied: 'The Egyptians you see today you will never see again' (Exod 14:13). And although it seems that they were not instantly consumed—they had after all spent at least twenty-four hours in hot pursuit of the Israelites—as soon as the eyes of the Holy Fire of God were turned upon them, the process of their destruction was initiated. They fell into confusion, panicked and died. Not one of them survived.

So, then, we have arrived at this electrifying conclusion: *Holy Fire consumes whatever is unholy, but protects, guides, motivates, empowers, liberates and brings God's presence and recognition to anything or anyone who is holy.* This is the chief characteristic of Holy Fire. It is not just a distinguished fire but a distinguishing fire; distinguishing the clean from the unclean. Holy Fire is not just a separate fire but a separating fire; separating the holy from the unholy; not merely passive, but powerfully active. It is the ultimate filter, removing the imperfection that cannot pollute the perfect holiness of God. If something is truly separated *for* God then first it must be separated *by* God. As we shall see later, such a fire is by its very nature a purifying fire, since the impure is automatically removed.

A consuming fire

When Moses was exhorting the Israelites to be careful not to forget the covenant they had made with the Lord—to worship him and him only—he warned them not to make any idols: 'For the Lord your God is a consuming fire, a jealous God' (Deut 4:24).

Moses, the one with whom God himself spoke face to face, clearly and not in riddles, knew his God. Moses had seen the wrath of God poured out in judgement and in Holy Fire on many occasions when his anger burned against the Israelites for their idolatry, their whining, their murmuring and their grumbling. God, who says, 'My Name is Jealous,' will consume everything and everyone who is not holy, because he is by nature holy. His fire is a demonstration and manifestation of his nature, so his fire is holy, and his fire is a consuming fire. It is the chief characteristic of it.

Once again in Hebrews 12 we are warned: 'See to it that you do not refuse him who speaks' (v. 25), that is the Lord, for 'our God is a consuming fire'. If we refuse God, or we refuse to listen to him, we understand neither his power nor his judgement. We dare not refuse him, but only stand in awe of both. 'It is a dreadful thing to fall into the hands of the living God' (Heb 10:31).

Here is a power so fierce that its very hovering created the world; a fire so hot that nothing and no person can stand in its presence unless deemed holy by God. Only then does the fire of God not consume. That is why, '"They will neither harm nor destroy on all my holy mountain," says the Lord' (Is 65:25), because it is a *holy* mountain, and those who dwell there shall be deemed to be holy (or rather *re*deemed). The fire of God shall not touch them, but rather it shall empower and glorify them. Praise God!

We begin to catch a glimpse, not only of the power of salvation, but the fundamental necessity of it. God is not playing party games. How could anyone be so presumptuous as to suggest that they could enter into the holy presence of God, except that first he declares them holy? All vain attempts by man to invent religions or methods for making themselves holy are shown to be totally ridiculous. God would not allow the builders of Babel to succeed in building something 'to reach to the heavens', and neither can he allow any similar efforts by man today to pull himself up by his bootstraps. This is not for his protection but for ours. One small mistake, one tiny blot of sin on the copybook of our soul, leads to instant destruction by the consuming fire should we approach the holy presence of God. This makes a nonsense too of any doctrine of a progressive salvation. We either are or we are not deemed holy. To be partly holy is clearly a ridiculous concept, leading inevitably to complete destruction.

So for the unholy, then, the fire of God is instant destruction, but it does not provide unconditional immunity to the sanctified.

A fatal mistake

Aaron must have been a very unusual man. Chosen by the
Lord almost by default through Moses' own fears, he was
not slow to accept his brother's challenge to help him take
up the leadership of Israel. He was saved from the
deserved destruction for his part in the golden calf deba-
cle by the intercession of this same brother. And after such
inauspicious beginnings, he went on to become the high
priest of the whole of Israel. His career could hardly be
described as exemplary. Nevertheless, here he was at the
top of the tree, together with his four sons.

These four, Nadab, Abihu, Eleazar and Ithamar, must
have been astonished observers. Here was their father,
admittedly an eloquent speaker but none the less of no
great account or prospects, catapulted into a position of
spiritual importance such as had never been recorded—
that of high priest of the holy and living God. And as far
as they could see, it was only by virtue of the 'accident'
of being Moses' brother! What birthright was this? And
more than that . . . *they* were to inherit it. What had they
done to deserve it? It seemed that they could do no
wrong. Father had built the golden calf, and look where
it led him! To the top of the tree! Nadab as the eldest
must have felt the glow of satisfaction swell in his breast
into a full-blown furnace of pride. They were to be
anointed to an eternal priesthood and would be the
future high priests of the all-powerful God for all generations. His family would control the tribes of Israel for
all time. Moses had had the chance, but had chosen not
to take it up. Very well then; Nadab would show them
who was in charge. He and his soul-mate brother bided
their time.

They had another reason for their inordinate vanity. On
the day of the reading of the Book of the Covenant, they

had, quite literally, seen God. Along with the seventy elders, they, as Aaron's sons, 'went up and saw the God of Israel' (Exod 24:9), and as it confirms two verses later, 'They saw God, and they ate and drank.' Surely it had been drummed into them from birth that anyone who looks upon God would die, and yet here they were, having been given that supreme privilege, and yet walking around scot free! They must have believed that they were immune to the power of the Holy Fire, and glowed with self-satisfaction. How special they felt—how superior to the others. It was only natural that they should be picked out to be priests.

The week of their ordination went by with great ceremony. They were very careful to follow exactly the rituals of the consecration. And then began their ministry—making offerings of atonement for the people. Their father Aaron lifted his hands towards the people and blessed them (Lev 9:22). Never had these sons imagined such greatness, such power. They were robed in glorious splendour; they were anointed with oil; they were sprinkled with the blood of sacrifice; they were ordained priests; they had power over the sins of the people. And as if to justify their newly exalted position, fire came out from the Lord and consumed the sacrifices. The people were in awe and worshipped the Lord. At last they were fully fledged priests of El-Shaddai. For Nadab and his brother Abihu the wait was over.

In full confidence of their new-found 'immunity', they completely misjudged the nature of the fire of God—that it is holy. So, as we read in Leviticus 10, they 'took their censers, put fire in them and added incense; and they offered unauthorised fire before the Lord, contrary to his command. So fire came out from the presence of the Lord and consumed them, and they died before the Lord' (Lev 10:1–2). I don't doubt that the whole community was

totally stunned. With supreme understatement the Bible
says, 'Aaron remained silent.'

What on earth had happened? What had they done that
was so much worse than their father's calf-building exer-
cise that it merited instant vaporisation? They were not the
only ones who had acted contrary to the Lord's command.
What was the significance of the incense and the censers,
if any, and what *was* the 'unauthorised fire'?

These questions lead us into other aspects of the Holy
Fire of God, which we shall examine in more detail in the
next chapters. For the moment, it is sufficient to note
Moses' explanation: 'Among those who approach me I
will show myself holy' (Lev 10:3). God, whose fire is
holy, consumes the unholy. As Moses later pointed out:
'You must distinguish between the holy and the common,
between the unclean and the clean' (Lev 10:10). For
whatever reason, Nadab and Abihu found themselves
unholy and unclean in the holy presence and the result
was inevitable. They were burned up.

There is another small detail which we shouldn't miss.
Moses called the cousins of the deceased to come and take
their remains outside the camp, for clearly God had
demonstrated that they were unclean. 'So they came and
carried them, still in their tunics, outside the camp, as
Moses ordered' (Lev 10:5). Here again the fire of God
discriminated between those to be judged, who were
consumed, and even their own tunics, which evidently
were not consumed! As one commentator so correctly
observes, 'Most unlikely!' But the Bible is clear.
Although obviously the bodies were not so destroyed as
to make their carrying impossible, the very mention of the
tunics at all is clearly signalling this discriminatory characteristic of God's consuming fire which we have already
seen in the fiery furnace, where the binding cords were
burned, but the clothes were not.

Why? Because the new priests and their tunics had just been consecrated and thus proclaimed holy by God. Now the men had sinned and attracted the wrath of the destructive power of the Holy Fire, while the tunics of course remained holy and so were not consumed!

God will demonstrate his holiness among those who approach him. As we approach him, not only will we become aware of his holiness, but others will see it also. Our very survival is a demonstration of our status before him should we survive by his grace! What fantastic assurance of salvation; that we can approach the holy presence of the living God, and not be vaporised!

It must have been little comfort to Aaron that his sons were not alone in suffering such judgement. In Numbers 11 we read of the complaints of the Israelites about unspecified hardships attracting similar judgement, this time consuming some of the outskirts of the camp. Once again, the intercession of Moses effected a reprieve. You would think that by now they would have been in holy fear of the Lord and his consuming fire, but not a bit of it.

Korah's New Age movement

Here comes Korah, a priest, proclaiming the philosophy of New Age: 'The whole community is holy, every one of them, and the Lord is with them. Why then do you set yourselves above the Lord's assembly?' (Num 16:3).

New Age philosophy, among other errors, teaches that since God is everywhere, he is in everything, therefore everything is holy. So, it is argued, since everyone is already holy, there is no such thing as sin, and no need of repentance. The natural consequence of this, as we see here, is rebellion against God's anointed, and finally destruction. This all happened three-and-a-half thousand years ago. There is nothing new about 'New Age'!

Korah's 250 followers were equally deceived. 'Who do you think you are?' they were asking Moses. Well, Moses was learning a thing or two. He had seen the fire of the Lord in action, and he knew that it was the fire of judgement, consuming what was unholy and protecting what was holy. But Korah and his lot didn't know the Lord, or at least if they did they were blinded by their rebellious attitude, and Moses knew it, so he set them a trap! Read about it in Numbers 16.

'Right,' says Moses, 'we'll see who is holy around here. Let the Lord be the judge!' He commands Korah and his renegades to fill their censers with fire (maybe Moses had just been writing Leviticus 10!) and offer it before the Lord, and see what happens. And he commands Aaron to bring his censer too, to show fair play, and prove the discriminating power of the Holy Fire. The glory of the Lord appears to the entire assembly, but still the rebels are not repentant. Moses prophesies their destruction and immediately Korah and his co-conspirators are swallowed up by the earth, and 'fire came out from the Lord and consumed the 250 men who were offering the incense' (Num 16:35).

All that was left was 'smouldering remains' and 'coals'. And the censers. Why the censers? Let us listen to the Lord's answer:

> Tell Eleazar son of Aaron, the priest, to take the censers out of the smouldering remains and scatter the coals some distance away, for the censers are holy—the censers of the men who sinned at the cost of their lives. Hammer the censers into sheets to overlay the altar, for they were presented before the Lord and have become holy. Let them be a sign to the Israelites (Num 16:37–38).

The censers were holy. The men who sinned at the cost of their lives were consumed, but the censers which were holy survived the judgement of the Holy Fire of God, and the reason is so that it will be a sign to the Israelites, and

of course to us—a sign that they survived the Holy Fire of
God *because* they were holy.

We see Holy Fire in action again in Judges 6. As a sign
to Gideon, the angel of the Lord touched the food Gideon
had brought him with his staff, and fire flared from the
rock and consumed it. Gideon must have been shocked,
but then realised that this was God's way of saying 'thank
you', and confirming Gideon's commission. It is note-
worthy that the rock apparently was not consumed, but
since the fire came *from* the rock, it was presumably holy.
This is even more evident in the story of Mount Carmel.

The God who answers by fire

Elijah was a man of legendary faith, who lived in truly
desperate times. King Ahab was the most evil Israelite
king ever to have lived, besides which he was married to
Jezebel, often considered the epitome, if not the authoress,
of witchcraft. Together they not only nearly brought about
the destruction of David's line of succession, but the
establishment of the worship of Baal throughout the
whole kingdom of Israel. Elijah found himself firmly set
against them, and no occasion was as dramatic as Elijah's
challenge to the prophets of Baal on Mount Carmel,
described in 1 Kings 18.

The story is well known. Elijah challenged the 450
prophets of Baal to set up a sacrifice, but not to put a
match to it, and to pray to Baal. He would do the same to
the Lord. And as he said to them: '''Then you call on the
name of your god, and I will call on the name of the Lord.
The god who answers by fire—he is God.'' Then all the
people said, ''What you say is good'' ' (1 Kings 18:24).

I doubt that many of us would risk our lives on such a
challenge, but Elijah knew his God. The Lord would not
allow Elijah to lose, because to do so would give glory to

Baal. Elijah knew he was on to a certainty. He was going
to have some fun at the expense of the Baalites! First they
were exhorted and then ridiculed for their 'frantic prophe-
sying' to get Baal to answer by fire. 'Baal' remained
unimpressed. Then Elijah, still thoroughly enjoying himself, starts to stack the odds against himself. Having built
an altar with the sacrifice on it and dug a trench around it,
he proceeds to drown it in gallons of water (and there was
a drought going on at the time)! He then calls briefly but
faithfully on the Lord: 'Let it be known today that you are
God in Israel' (1 Kings 18:36).

Two verses later God answers: 'Then the fire of the Lord
fell and burned up the sacrifice, the wood, the stones and
the soil, and also licked up the water in the trench' (v. 38).

Not only did God demonstrate his existence, he showed
his power; that he answers prayer; that he is the God of Israel,
but also the God of fire (and therefore of the whole of
creation); that he is a God who allows repentance (see verse
37), but also a God of judgement. He accepts the sacrifice.
But far more than that. He accepts his prophet, but totally
rejects the heathen prophets, descendants of Israel though
they may be. Their fate was soon sealed. Meanwhile, let us
note that the Holy Fire of God burned up not just the
sacrifice, but also the wood, the stones, the soil and the
water as well. Why? Because they were not holy. Elijah
had never consecrated the altar. It is a miracle, even a
mystery, that the prophets of Baal survived the flash of
fire, but perhaps they had anticipated trouble and were well
out of the way. However, their destruction was imminent.

In this chapter we have seen that Holy Fire is essentially
destructive to every unholy person or thing, but positive
and creative to the holy. We have seen sacrifices, and
people, consumed by Holy Fire. And we have seen
bushes and censers remain. The story does not end
there. We are only just opening the door of discovery.

3

Holy Fire and Holy Sacrifice

When God showed up on Mount Carmel, he was demonstrating, among other things, his acceptance of the sacrifice and, by inference, of his people who were offering the sacrifice.

We see the same sort of thing in 1 Chronicles 21:26. David had fallen into trouble when, against the Lord's will, he decided to count his fighting men, and had set up a sacrifice on the threshing floor of Araunah. God showed his forgiveness by answering with fire from heaven. Again, when Solomon had finished building the temple, and had completed his prayer of dedication, 'fire came down from heaven and consumed the burnt offering and the sacrifices' (2 Chron 7:1).

God seems to be showing his approval in each of these cases, but there is much more to it than that. God is actually getting involved with the process of sacrifice, and as we begin to understand the nature of Holy Fire, we can begin to see more clearly the reasons behind this involvement. This will also help us to see better what was actually happening at the moment of Christ's death. So let us try to look in a little more detail at the purpose of sacrifice, and apply our new understanding to it. In order to do this, we shall need to dig into the turgid depths of the book of Leviticus, but it is actually fascinating what can be found there.

In Leviticus 10:10 Moses warns us to learn to distinguish between the holy and the common, between the unclean and the clean. Until now we have considered 'holy' and 'clean', and 'unholy' and 'unclean' to be synonymous. In fact something that is holy is something set apart for the Lord, or dedicated exclusively to the Lord.

From the story so far, we have seen that anything unclean could hardly be set apart for the Lord since it would end up consumed! That is certainly the case, but as we look at the purpose of sacrifice, we see that the unclean can, for a brief moment at least, be holy. How can this be?

The destruction of Aaron's sons Nadab and Abihu took place after their elaborate ordination ceremony initiating them as priests, and after the beginning of their ministry. They had offered the various sacrifices required of them by Moses, and Aaron had stepped down and gone into the tent with Moses. When they came out, the glory of the Lord had appeared to the people.

Then we read in Leviticus 9:24, 'Fire came out from the presence of the Lord and consumed the burnt offering and the fat portions on the altar.'

It has been suggested by some scholars that this verse of Scripture was added at a much later date, in order to emphasise the Lord's acceptance of the process of sacrifice, of the ordination rituals which had now been completed, and of the priests themselves in their newly consecrated state. It is argued that this must be the case, since the various offerings and fat portions had *already* been burned by Aaron and that the later editor had 'missed' this point!

Personally I do not believe that even had the verse been a later editor's addition he would have been so careless, nor in fact that Scripture, by whomever it may have been written, makes such errors! No, there is a deeper truth here.

It is true that the preceding verses give us a clear

chronology. For example, in verses 22 and 23 we read that 'having sacrificed the sin offering . . . [Aaron] stepped down. Moses and Aaron then went into the Tent of Meeting. When they came out . . . the glory of the Lord appeared.' So the glory of the Lord appeared *after* the completion of the ceremony. But verse 24 is not chronologically tied to these verses, and seems to be added by way of explanation. However, the sacrifices have already been made, so the fire cannot be consuming them again! So we are led to ask: If this is an explanation, what is it of?

In Leviticus 1:7, the Lord clearly instructs Moses that the sons of Aaron are to place the fire on the altar, and interestingly we nowhere read that this was done by them during the ordination ceremony. Since this ceremony is described in such minute detail, this would be a surprising omission, and it seems clear that verse 24 is an explanation of where the fire on the altar had come from; that is, supernaturally from the Lord, rather than through the normal channels. Instead of fire being placed there by Aaron's sons, the offerings presented throughout the ceremony were consumed by the Holy Fire of the Lord rather than by natural fire, as had been the case so far whenever Moses, rather than Aaron or his sons, had offered sacrifices.

It may seem curious that God should command them to place the natural fire on the altar, and later do it supernaturally himself instead. But there is a precedent to this type of behaviour when he commanded Abraham to sacrifice Isaac, but eventually provided the sacrifice himself. Isaac lived because God intervened. In the same way, God provided the fire of sacrifice supernaturally. Why is this so important?

Now we know the effect of the Holy Fire of God upon the holy and the unholy, we can see more clearly what the

Lord is trying to show us in three different aspects of these offerings.

Acceptance

The Lord is indeed demonstrating his acceptance of them as offerings far more clearly than had the fire been natural fire, by being intimately involved. God has always been involved in the affairs of man, going to the ultimate involvement on the cross.

First, everything belongs to the Lord, and anything we offer back to him was always his to do what he willed with anyway. David understood this when he thanked the Lord for the gifts towards the building of the temple: 'But who am I, and who are my people, that we should be able to give as generously as this? Everything comes from you, and we have given you only what comes from your hand' (1 Chron 29:14).

And now God is going beyond his declaration in Psalm 50:8 when he says, 'I do not rebuke you for your sacrifices or your burnt offerings, which are ever before me.' He is actually *taking part* in the process of offering; taking the offerings back to himself as it were, proclaiming that they are indeed an 'aroma pleasing to the Lord'.

The importance of this is that by such involvement in the process of sacrifice, God renders meaningless the pagan concept of appeasement. This is so beloved of other religions, which may understand the fear of some remote, unapproachable or terrifying God, but since they do not know him, do not understand his love. His are the cattle on a thousand hills, so how on earth will their slaughter and offering back to him appease him, since he made them alive, not dead, and since their death is ultimately always in his hands anyway? And how can you appease someone who is actively involved in the very act of appeasement?

Secondly, God's supernatural intervention in the work of the priesthood is an important reminder that the priesthood is actually his—'You are a priest for ever, in the order of Melchizedek' (Ps 110:4), and that he now accepts the Aaronic priesthood, but again with a supernatural reminder that the power belongs to the Lord, and not the priests; that it is a delegated authority. Although the principle of the Aaronic priesthood was fundamentally important to the Israelite ritual, and is still to our understanding of the priesthood of Jesus himself, it is crucial to understand also that it is a subjected priesthood—that is, one of service rather than of dominion. Whenever in later history this principle was forgotten, be it in Palestine during the Roman occupation, or even later in the church of Rome, the priesthood became corrupt.

Even within the church today structures can be found which emphasise the elevation and authority of the priest or pastor, thus diminishing the true role of a servant delegated to minister in the power of God by his grace alone. The tendency lingers to worship the signs and wonders, and praise the minister through whom God works, rather than ascribing all glory and power to God.

Communion

There is in every act of worship, whether it be sacrificial or some other form of adoration, a desire on the part of the worshipper for communion with God. This is that deep-seated God-given heart for fellowship with our Creator that God first breathed into man in Eden when he gave man life, and which is the prime motivating force leading us to seek him out before we know him—that inner spiritual hollow which all the indulgences of life leave

unanswered and unassuaged. When Jesus said that the
Sabbath was made for man, not man for the Sabbath, he
was addressing this primordial need of ours—we were
born to be worshippers and to enjoy communion or
fellowship with the living God.

The more astonishing thing is that God himself equally
desires that same fellowship with us. Feel the desperate
sense of loss that God betrays in the Garden of Eden, in
the cool of the day, when he cries from his wounded heart,
'Adam, where are you?' This heart-cry of God comes not
merely from his knowledge that now Christ would have to
die, but from the tragic loneliness of one losing the
intimate fellowship of his friend.

How much more poignant is our understanding of God's
desire for this relationship with his people when we see
him assisting them in their attempts to honour him through
their sacrifice. It is as though God in his love cannot keep
away, but must somehow take part himself, so anxious is
he to enjoy their company. There is an intimacy in his
action which belies the awesomeness of the event itself.
How wonderful, how demonstrable his love.

Substitution

The third aspect of God's divine participation in these
offerings is that the principle of atonement is fundamental to God's provision for mankind since his fall. It is
never the efforts of man himself that bring justification
before God, but always God's provision of a means of
atonement: 'For the life of a creature is in the blood, and *I
have given it to you* to make atonement for yourselves on
the altar; it is the blood that makes atonement for one's
life' (Lev 17:11, my emphasis).

God provides the means, and when the fire of God
comes down and consumes the sacrifices offered by the

high priest, God is not just participating in the sacrifice by the provision of the means of atonement in the first place, but by actually being the means of their destruction. He is declaring the sacrifices to be unclean, since they are demonstrably consumed by his Holy Fire, which as we have seen only happens to the unclean!

Surely, though, an acceptable sacrifice must be holy—that is, be set apart for the Lord? Yes! But the very fact that the offering should be unblemished is essential if it is to be a substitute for that which is blemished—ourselves. The unblemished sacrifice is deemed to be blemished by taking upon itself the sinfulness of man, and in so doing becomes unholy or unclean at the point of its death, just as Jesus cried, 'My God, my God, why have you forsaken me?' at that moment, allowing the previously unclean (us) to be deemed clean, or holy. At that point, the holy sacrifice becomes unclean, and then of course cannot survive. Jesus, for whom the fire of God was a constant part of his nature, bringing power and fellowship with the Father and protection and guidance, now finds in that awful instant that the same Holy Fire is his destruction.

During the initiation ceremony of Aaron this discriminatory power is emphasised once again by the fact that the altar itself *did* survive, and this in the face of the supernaturally hot Holy Fire of God. But of course the altar had just been consecrated (Lev 8:15), so it was holy. Therefore, no amount of Holy Fire would destroy it. Once again we see the specific nature of Holy Fire—leaving the holy, but consuming the unholy.

The fact that we read in Exodus 29:37 that 'the altar will be most holy, and whatever touches it will be holy', makes no difference. Of course the sacrifice was holy, ie, set apart for the Lord. But at the crucial moment, God demonstrates that it becomes unholy, or rather unclean, because he deems it to be unclean, in order that it may substitute for the sins of the Israelites.

And this is the whole point about the death of Jesus himself, who had to be perfect for his substitutionary death to make any sense at all. If *he* had been sinful, he would first have had to die for his own sins before he could die for ours, and then could not have risen from the dead, since he would have deserved his own death. So God the Son took an intimate part in the offering, by being (providing) the sacrifice, and God the Father took an intimate part by being the means of the death of Jesus (by, at the last possible moment, deeming him unclean), just as he was the means of the destruction of the sacrifices offered by Aaron the high priest. God was showing us the divine principle, and preparing the way for his own substitutionary death, when the High Priest himself, Jesus Christ, offered the ultimate sacrifice on the cross. Thanks be to the Father that this sacrifice was not, nor could be, permanently consumed, but rose again from the dead on the third day, and sits as the great High Priest at the right hand of the Almighty!

This too is why God chose to wait until this moment—the commencement of the ministry of the high priest—to manifest himself in Holy Fire, in order to highlight the importance of the role of the high priest, and to bring a prophetic precedent to the divine power of the High Priest Jesus, of whom John the Baptist said, 'He will baptise you with the Holy Spirit and with fire.' We are soon coming to that.

Had God not been the means of destruction of the sacrifices offered by Aaron and his sons, we might have remained unclear about the inevitability, the divine purpose and the divine method, of the destruction of such a sacrifice. As it is, God proclaims with no room for doubt the inescapability of the 'consuming fire'.

4

Authorised Fire

So we see that God gets involved in sacrifice. Therefore the high priest who offered the sacrifices had to be very careful not to get consumed. It was vital for him to understand the principles of the Holy Fire. This knowledge of the nature of Holy Fire acts as a magnifying glass for us also, to aid our understanding of God's plan for the priesthood, and especially for Jesus himself.

How true it is that we only seem to learn from our mistakes, but I praise the Lord that he has given us the opportunity to learn from those of others too! We now need to try to do just that by picking up a loose end that we left in Chapter 2. Then we can move on to one of the most glorious truths of the Holy Fire of God in the next chapter.

We left Nadab and Abihu believing that they were now, upon gaining their new status, deemed to be holy by the Lord, and that they could move with impunity. Their destruction proved otherwise, but where exactly did they go wrong?

They had, like so many others since, misunderstood the difference between holiness and ordination, or even between holiness and anointing. King Saul, chosen of the Lord and anointed by Samuel, displayed the collapse of a life through pride and disobedience, even to the consulting of mediums, and yet remained 'the Lord's anointed' until his death—a fact recognised by David, and which cost the Amalekite his life in 2 Samuel 1. How often too have we watched heart-

broken as certain Christian leaders today, clearly greatly
gifted, have failed to withstand the worldly pressures of
such leadership, losing their holiness—their being 'dedicated to the Lord'—and falling so tragically under the with-
ering cross-fire of the hypocritical machine-guns of the
world's media.

First, it is just possible that Aaron's sons had been
drunk at the time of the unauthorised fire experience,
since the Lord tells Aaron seemingly out of the blue in
Leviticus 10:9 that they should not drink fermented drink
when they go into the Tent of Meeting, or they would die.

Secondly, they went in before the Lord to offer incense,
which only Aaron had been given permission to do at this
stage. The offering of incense throughout Scripture is a
'type' or symbol for prayer (eg, Rev 5:8), and was to be
the duty of the high priest, especially on the Day of
Atonement, when atonement was made for Israel. On
that day, in fact, Aaron was to 'take a censer full of
burning coals from the altar before the Lord and two
handfuls of finely ground fragrant incense and take them
behind the curtain. He is to put the incense on the fire
before the Lord, and the smoke of the incense will conceal
the atonement cover above the Testimony, so that he will
not die' (Lev 16:12–13).

From this we may learn that prayer, or symbolically
incense, may shield us from the destructive power of the
glory of God, but that this prayer needs to be offered by the
high priest alone, and in the right circumstances only; that is,
after his sanctification. Once again, God in his mighty provision has given us Jesus as our High Priest, who 'is at the right
hand of God and is also interceding for us' (Rom 8:34).

Incense was regularly offered to other gods and on other
altars—for example, Isaiah mentions brick ones—and on
high places and under spreading trees, as part of the
worship rituals, just as it is used today in Hinduism,

Confucianism and so on. In the temple of God, Solomon offered incense routinely (1 Kings 9:25), even though he was not a priest, and he was not consumed, although King Uzziah of Judah took it upon himself to burn incense in 2 Chronicles 26, and contracted leprosy for his trouble. However, it is made clear that his judgement was for his pride and his attitude rather than just for the offering of incense. So it seems unlikely that Aaron's two eldest sons died merely because they offered incense, even though they were not obeying the letter of the regulations.

Furthermore, later on in Leviticus 10 Aaron incurs the wrath of Moses because his two remaining sons make another elementary mistake—remember that all these regulations were brand new to the people, and they didn't have years of tradition or experience to fall back on. This time Aaron, in some exasperation I have no doubt, pleads his cause with Moses, who understands the extenuating circumstances and lets him off. Once again God makes it clear that although the letter of the law is important, it is the attitude of its adherents that is more important—a fact that Jesus himself was quick enough to point out: 'Woe to you, teachers of the law and Pharisees, you hypocrites! You give a tenth of your spices—mint, dill and cummin. But you have neglected the more important matters of the law—justice, mercy and faithfulness. You should have practised the latter, without neglecting the former' (Mt 23:23).

No, we are looking for more than simple inadvertent law-breaking; more even than over-indulgence in fermented drinks, though neither is condoned. The deaths of Aaron's sons are mentioned several times in the Bible, and almost always reference is made to the offering of unauthorised fire—it is this which caused their downfall. We have alluded to their probable attitude before, and it seems certain that these two had hearts full of pride. We cannot treat the presence of the Lord lightly, as Moses pointed out to Aaron in Leviticus 16:2: 'The Lord said to Moses: "Tell your brother Aaron not to come whenever he chooses into the Most Holy Place behind the curtain in front of the atonement cover on the ark, or else he will die, because I appear in the cloud over the atonement cover." '

First of all, then, Nadab and Abihu approached the Lord with a wrong attitude—one of pride. This in itself is enough to warrant the judgement of God. The fact that they were now ordained priests made it worse, because God expects a higher standard of behaviour among his anointed priests, as we see for example in reference to the appointment of bishops and deacons in Paul's first letter to Timothy.

However, I believe that the key is still the unauthorised fire. This strange expression is emphasised and is therefore vital. Perhaps the two sons went to the altar to collect fire for their censers, but being Holy Fire they were consumed as soon as they touched it. But this seems unlikely because we read that they did in fact put the fire in their censers, put in the incense, and actually offered it before the Lord. Also, their bodies were removed from 'the front of the sanctuary' (Lev 10:4) and not from in front of the altar. Again, we are told that the consuming fire 'came out from the presence of the Lord', that is, the sanctuary, and not from the altar. It seems therefore that it was not until they were in the process of offering the unauthorised fire that the trouble began.

We have seen that the Lord miraculously provided the fire for the sacrifices, overtaking the natural fire and replacing it with supernatural fire. This supernatural fire was therefore now the fire of God's purpose for sacrifice; that is, the authorised fire. Among other reasons, Nadab and Abihu were presumably afraid of such a powerful manifestation of the presence of God, and refused to risk handling it. They evidently therefore went to another source of fire other than the altar where God's Holy Fire was now burning, and that natural fire was the unauthorised fire that we read about. And just as the flash of Holy Fire killed the soldiers who tossed Shadrach, Meshach and Abednego into the flames, so now the Holy Fire of God came out from the presence of the Lord and consumed these two.

Contrast this with the angel of Revelation 8, with his golden censer, who filled it with fire *from the altar*. This is specifically mentioned in Scripture so that there could be no doubt that the angel was using authorised fire, the supernatural Holy Fire of God's judgement. This is hurled to the earth, bringing about the judgements of the seven trumpets upon the earth, one-third of which was devoured by this consuming fire at just the first of them.

However, Nadab and Abihu had another reason for choosing unauthorised fire—one much more serious and much more sinister, which deserved the full judgement of the wrath of God.

Through our new understanding of the vital ingredient, the authorised fire, we begin now to see the extent of their sin. Not only were they full of pride, they were ordained priests; it seems they had schemes of their own which I don't doubt included the usurping of power for themselves; but they intended to do it with no help from God. They deliberately rejected using the Holy Fire of God, preferring the natural to the supernatural. They wanted no part of God's miraculous intervention in their lives and ministry. Despite God's demonstration of his new way, they wanted to revert back to the old pagan methods, which elevated the position of the priest, and denied the presence of God himself. They preferred the privilege to the responsibility. They wanted the rank but not the risk.

Let us learn the lesson from their error. *We dare not deny the miraculous power of the fire of God today*. Let us minister not with the unauthorised fire of our own efforts, rituals or ambitions, but with the authorised fire of God, in fear and trembling.

They wanted to use their position for their own glory and not for God's. We have already shown how intimately God wanted to be involved with the sacrifices that his people made, and why. Nadab and Abihu were deliberately trying to cut God out of this involvement with the sacrifices. Had they been allowed to continue, God would have been condoning man's own efforts to reconcile himself with God instead of confessing the utter necessity of God's provision and involvement. It is the Old Testament equivalent of what so many people say today: 'We don't need Jesus; we can make it on our own.' This thinking is ultimately the root deception of all other religions.

That Satan should have attempted this same deception at such a crucial moment, the establishment of the priesthood, is typical. It would have completely negated the whole provision of the law by undermining the very authority of the priesthood set up by the law to administer that same law. The law would then be based upon the natural instead of the supernatural; upon ritual instead of worship; upon the will of man instead of the will of God.

Furthermore, those with a rebellious attitude towards God cannot live with the threat of his judgement, and the Holy Fire pronounces just that. For these fated two, then, this fire had to be disdained in favour of fire that could be brought under the subjection of man's will.

Nadab and Abihu were bent on the ultimate rebellion against God—to deliberately take all the privileges God had given, and to use them for their own ends, not only without acknowledging God's participation in their rise to power, but also denying and even attempting to exclude his power. This is exactly what Satan had done himself. No wonder he wanted to reproduce the event within God's priesthood.

Thank God that the Holy Fire intervened!

5

A Baptism by Fire

The flaming sword

For thousands of years God had waited for this moment. Since the fall of man he had been saving up his blessings for the great triumph—keeping his powder dry, almost literally!

In the Garden of Eden, God's 'great gamble' appeared to have failed. He had created the world in order to found a fellowshipper. He had made his creature in his own image, and invested him with his own breath, the Spirit of life breathed into his nostrils. He had blessed him with his greatest blessing—'Be fruitful'—and had commanded him with his greatest command: 'You are free. . . .' He had provided the perfect environment, and he had defined the boundaries of his freedom with but one restriction (for all true freedom must have boundaries, or it becomes a free-for-all; strength must have structure)—he was not to eat of the tree of the knowledge of good and evil. And in God's understanding of his own desire for companionship, he had created for man woman.

Now together they had passed up their opportunity to eat of the tree of life (for that had not been denied them), and instead had done the only thing that could have separated them from God. They had disobeyed his command, and had sinned. God's great plan of love, for love always involves risk, seemed to have gone wrong.

It is not as if God wanted to curse them. In fact that curse was a kind of protection. True fellowship with God was now an impossibility since it would lead to destruction. As we have seen, the Holy Fire of his presence would be fatal to sinful man. But God's righteousness necessitated judgement of sin, and with the curse, God's emergency plan—his desperate, extreme but crucial emergency plan—was initiated. Immediately, the death of Jesus became a dreadful inevitability. Meanwhile, God had to make provision to retrieve the situation with a 'holding operation'. The curse pronounced judgement, but at the same time still left man an opportunity to be redeemed during his shortened lifetime, should he respond to God's love.

But he couldn't be allowed to remain in the garden, where he still had access to the tree of life. Had he eaten of it after the Fall, his judgement and his destruction would have been eternal and irrevocable—the tree imparting eternal life to man who at the same time was sinful could only mean one end: eternal destruction. God wanted a way that might enable man to be saved from such a disaster. That way was now to be unveiled, but in the meantime, man must be driven out of the garden, which was immediately protected by a flaming sword—'the sword of the Spirit, which is the word of God' (Eph 6:17). The Holy Fire of God, the consuming fire, the guardian of the tree of life, is as we have already seen the agent by which God sorts the holy from the unholy.

The entrance to the garden, and the tree of life which is there, is still guarded by this flaming sword! The two-edged sword which issues from the mouth of God is his Word. For man to find eternity, he must first come through his Word, which is Jesus. Jesus himself said, 'I am the

gate'—the entry to the garden, the garden of fellowship
with God, the garden of divine provision, the garden of
divine purpose, the garden of beauty, the garden of the
tree of life from which man had been banished.

And now at last the wait was over. But before we see
how and why the Holy Fire of God was such a vital part of
this new plan, we must first look at God's methods to
understand better what he was about to do.

A covenant sign

After the fall of man, God continued to look for obedience
in his erstwhile friend. Time and time again he made
agreements, covenants, proving his own faithfulness,
never failing to keep his word, waiting endlessly, usually
in vain, for man to respond equally.

Each time God made such an agreement, he sealed the
covenant with a sign. God's first covenant with man was
made with Noah and all living creatures after the flood,
declaring that the everlasting sign of that covenant would
be the rainbow. It was a covenant of life; an eternal
promise of protection.

He made a covenant with Abraham that his seed should
be as the grains of sand or as the stars in the sky, and the
sign of his covenant was the sign of circumcision.
Through Moses he made the Old Covenant, or Old Testament, and the sign of his covenant was the sabbath day. He
made a covenant with David, that he would have a
descendant on the throne for ever, which was and is the
sign itself! And Jesus himself is the fulfilment of this
covenant, as he sits at the right hand of the Father for ever.

Now God needed a sign of his New Covenant with man.
We have seen that God is always intimately involved in
the affairs of man, and now comes the ultimate demonstration of his purpose. When God first breathed his life-

giving Spirit into Adam at the creation, he was laying
down his divine principle for life, the indwelling of his
Holy Spirit. This was always God's intention for his
people. But after the Fall, God was unable to fulfil his
purpose for man, for such an indwelling, as we have seen,
would have been totally destructive. First the newly
entered sin-element must be dealt with and removed.
Only then could he bring to fulfilment his great design.

God's sign of the New Covenant is not the cross, though
it has been pointed out that that is Christ's unique logo.
Indeed it is, but it is not ours. Nor is this sign the blood of
Jesus, though the mark of the blood is part of the inheritance of every believer. Neither is the covenant sign the
Lord's Supper, or Holy Communion, which is a sacrament, not a sign. No, *the covenant sign of the New
Testament is the baptism of the Holy Spirit*. 'Having
believed, you were marked in him with a seal, the promised Holy Spirit, who is a deposit guaranteeing our
inheritance until the redemption of those who are God's
possession—to the praise of his glory' (Eph 1:13b–14).

Just as the betrothed wears the gift of her engagement
ring as a reminder and demonstration to the world of her
promised marriage, so the Holy Spirit himself is the seal,
the covenant sign, which guarantees our inheritance. How
does the Holy Spirit act as the guarantee? How can Paul
state this so categorically? And what is the significance of
this in relation to the unfolding of our story? It is one of
the most exciting discoveries we can make in our Christian life.

Fire that separated

John the Baptist describes Jesus as the one who will
'baptise you with the Holy Spirit and with fire' (Mt
3:11). In saying that he, John, must become less, while

Jesus becomes greater, John was really saying that rather than himself, we should call Jesus the Baptist! It is Jesus to whom we should turn for this new baptism.

And later, after his death and resurrection, having disarmed the powers and authorities; having become the substitutionary Lamb of sacrifice; having taken the sins of the world upon himself so that the world could be deemed to be holy; having broken the curse of God in the Garden of Eden and removed the reason for man's banishment from the tree of life, Jesus himself promises, 'You will be baptised with the Holy Spirit!' Why?

Because now the reason for God withholding his hand is gone. God's people can now be deemed to be holy through the cross. Now that the unholy have been deemed to be holy, there is no risk of their destruction by the Holy Fire of God. The flaming sword need flash its warning no longer. God's people are redeemed by the blood of Jesus. Therefore God can pour out his Holy Spirit with impunity.

This is why an unbeliever, one who is not 'washed in the blood of the Lamb', one who retains the unholiness and uncleanliness of the world, cannot possibly be baptised in the Holy Spirit. It would mean instant destruction. It is not because God is being miserly or even discriminatory with his blessings. God longs to bless each and every person, of whatever race, religion or philosophy, with all the fullness of his Holy Spirit, but cannot because it would not mean blessing but destruction. God is constrained by compassion. It is for their preservation that God withholds his hand from pouring out the mighty power of his Spirit—his consuming fire—upon unbelievers. Without being deemed holy, none would survive.

The promise is for all those who believe: 'He redeemed us in order that the blessing given to Abraham might come to the Gentiles through Christ Jesus, so that by faith we

might receive the promise of the Spirit' (Gal 3:14). This is
God's purpose of salvation: that this indwelling, this ful-
filling, intimate fellowship with him is fully restored for
ever.

And this is what the baptism of the Holy Spirit means.
When God's flame, the Holy Fire of God, touched the
heads of the disciples in the Upper Room, God was
marking them with the seal of the New Covenant. With
each individual flame separating over each individual
head, God is declaring, 'I deem this one to be holy in
my sight,' and the next flame, 'I deem this one holy,' and
the next, 'This one is holy,' and the next, 'Holy', and the
next, and the next. Over each and every believer who
believes and receives, God declares: 'Holy!' Oh, what a
wonderful truth!

The reason why this baptism is a guarantee of our
inheritance is because we are not destroyed. We have
seen the Lord and have lived! Greater than this, we have
been allowed past the cherubim and the flaming sword,
and eaten the fruit from the tree of life. God's fire
separated and marked each one individually. The baptism
of the Holy Spirit is not just a sign to the whole body of
Christ, but to individuals. Each one is declared and
demonstrated to be holy in God's sight.

When Christ returns we shall be caught up with him,
and the perishable will become imperishable. Then we
shall no longer be in need of a guarantee—as the
betrothed wears her engagement ring. Then the bride of
Christ will already be wearing her wedding garments, and
the veil will already be lifted from her face. Then she will
look into the eyes of her Husband, Jesus, and see him face
to face for the first time, exactly as he really is. But until
that glorious return, when Christ takes his bride for
himself, we have a divine promise of marriage, sealed
with the Holy Spirit. His presence within (and upon) our

perishable bodies, *his unconsuming presence*, is the perfect guarantee that we have indeed been changed; that we are already a new creation awaiting the final moment of his promise.

Let me affirm at once that I am not saying that if we have not received the baptism of the Holy Spirit we are not saved. What I am saying is that only once we are saved can we receive the baptism of the Holy Spirit. And the baptism of the Holy Spirit proves that we are saved, because without salvation we would be destroyed. Of course it is possible to be saved without receiving the baptism of the Holy Spirit; millions are. But God's ultimate desire is for all to be baptised in this way, because without it we lack the New Covenant sign and the consequent wonderful assurance of salvation that this baptism brings: 'We know that we live in him and he in us, because he has given us of his Spirit' (1 Jn 4:13).

For a sign to be a sign at all, it must be demonstrably visible, not only to the bearer of the sign, but also to others. This is why the baptism of the Holy Spirit is accompanied by the gift of tongues—so that the one baptised may have that blessed assurance of his own salvation, just as the betrothed may gaze lovingly at the ring, not just for its beauty which may be great, but for the relationship it represents which is greater. And also that the world may know that this believer is chosen, set apart by God, to be part of his bride, the church.

There is a warning implicit in the sign too. Other would-be suitors are warned off. 'No!' the sign says. 'This one is already promised! You must take your suit elsewhere.' Thus I believe is the power of the gift of tongues when confronting the powers of darkness. Satan has no authority here, for this one belongs to God, and here is the sign to prove it! It is not the tongues themselves that keep the devil away. It is the relationship which their manifestation represents. It is not us he is afraid of, but Jesus and the power of the Holy Spirit. Being unholy, he knows what the effect will be if he gets too close. Oh Christian, have the assurance of the effect of this power within you upon the enemy! The Holy Spirit is far too hot for the devil to handle. When we walk in the anointing and power of the Holy Spirit, demons will have to flee or else be destroyed by the Holy Fire.

What of those Christians who do not wear this precious gift, this engagement ring of the Holy Ghost?

For the duration of their time in the desert, the Israelites were not circumcised, even though God had established it as a sign to his people. So when they arrived at Gilgal, having crossed the Jordan into the Promised Land, God commanded Joshua to circumcise his people before they went into battle. But even through the deprivations (and the rebellions) of the desert, they remained God's chosen people. The title was never lost, despite their being uncircumcised. *It was not the sign which qualified them, but the promise.* So it is with us. It is the promise of God received by faith, that we are saved by the blood of Jesus, that makes us Christians. But having been chosen, it is his desire that we should carry his engagement ring. What betrothed does not desire her ring? And what betrothed, upon receiving her precious ring, does not wear it for all to see, with that inner warmth of pride, not in herself, but in the one to whom she is promised? And what soldier entering battle does not take up his sword—the flaming sword of the Holy Spirit?

However, unlike the Israelites of the Old Testament, God's chosen are no longer merely one tribe. Not only does God pour out his Spirit individually, but on the same Day of Pentecost he reminds us that this promise is for all flesh. For millennia, God's Holy Spirit came upon rare individuals, prophets or leaders, chosen of the Lord for a unique task, deemed by his sovereign grace therefore to be holy, in order to be equipped for the purpose of God to be fulfilled.

Now God was doing a new thing. Through the atoning sacrifice of Jesus, through the cleansing of his blood, suddenly the promise is for you and your children and all who are far off—for all whom the Lord our God will call. So it is today—the promise doesn't die! No word of God will pass away, and no promise either.

6

The Character of Holy Fire

God demonstrates his character through his Holy Fire. Now we see that since the Holy Spirit *is* his Holy Fire, it is inevitable that the character of God himself shines through. Earlier we traced some of these characteristics, and said that they were hauntingly familiar. God's grand design takes shape before our eyes.

Divine presence, guidance, freedom, protection, motivation and power, recognition or identification, discriminatory power; all these were identified as characteristics of the Holy Fire as it (or should I now say 'he'?) was manifested in the pages of the Old Testament. Now we see them brought to fulfilment through the outpouring of the Holy Spirit in the New.

Divine presence

God's divine presence dwelling within us, made possible by his glorious provision through the death and resurrection of Jesus, is the great and eternal truth of the gospel. Diplomatic relations have been restored. The usurping government of Satan has been ousted. God has an ambassador in our territory—the Holy Spirit, and we have one in his, Jesus.

Jesus declared that he would be with us *as* the Holy Spirit 'alway, even unto the end of the world. Amen' (Mt

28:20, KJV). This presence is a promise, and God is faithful. Just as the pillar of fire never left the Israelites, so, as we read in Nehemiah, God sends his Holy Spirit: 'Because of your great compassion you did not abandon them in the desert. By day the pillar of cloud did not cease to guide them on their path, nor the pillar of fire by night to shine on the way they were to take. You gave your good Spirit to instruct them' (Neh 9:19–20). He is there, day and night—during the good times and the bad times. (The story of the footsteps in the sand is rightly popular.) Indeed one of the very names of God is *Jehovah Shamma*, meaning 'God who is there'.

Sometimes I think God must get exasperated with his children when in our prayers we constantly plead, 'Oh God, be with us!' as we meet together, as we undertake some project, as we face uncertainty or crisis. Do we really need to pray this? It is surely faithless to continue to pray for what God has already promised to provide! His presence is guaranteed. No, rather let us thank him for it, and move on to things we *do* need to pray for. Let us stand by faith upon the certainty of his presence at least.

John 14.26

Guidance

The one whom Jesus called the Counsellor, who would 'teach you all things' (Jn 14:26) and 'guide you into all truth' (Jn 16:13) can be none other than the pillar of fire sent to guide God's people to the Promised Land. The Holy Spirit living within us acts as our guide through the desert. In the same way that the law of the Old Testament came to the Israelites from out of the fire, so now God promises 'to put my law in their minds and write it on their hearts' (Jer 31:33) by the indwelling fire of the Holy Spirit.

Would that we had the same discipline as our fore-fathers whose indiscretions have been well advertised

throughout Scripture, but who nevertheless obeyed faithfully the leading of the cloud and fire:

> On the day the tabernacle, the Tent of the Testimony, was set
> up, the cloud covered it. From evening till morning the cloud
> above the tabernacle looked like fire. That is how it continued
> to be; the cloud covered it, and at night it looked like fire.
> Whenever the cloud lifted from above the Tent, the Israelites
> set out; wherever the cloud settled, the Israelites encamped.
> At the Lord's command the Israelites set out, and at his
> command they encamped. As long as the cloud stayed over
> the tabernacle, they remained in camp. When the cloud
> remained over the tabernacle a long time, the Israelites
> obeyed the Lord's order and did not set out (Num 9:15–19).

And so it continues to verse 23:

> Sometimes the cloud was over the tabernacle only a few days;
> at the Lord's command they would encamp, and then at his
> command they would set out. Sometimes the cloud stayed
> only from evening till morning, and when it lifted in the
> morning, they set out. Whether by day or by night, whenever
> the cloud lifted, they set out. Whether the cloud stayed over
> the tabernacle for two days or a month or a year, the Israelites
> would remain in camp and not set out; but when it lifted, they
> would set out. At the Lord's command they encamped, and at
> the Lord's command they set out. They obeyed the Lord's
> order, in accordance with his command through Moses.

At times I think that the Holy Spirit's guidance to us
resembles more of a cloud upon our lives than the fire
of God. So often we try to move when he is staying still,
and vice versa. In our twentieth-century impatience, I
believe that the hardest command of the Holy Spirit to
obey is simply 'wait'. How long can be the gestation
period of the Holy Spirit's plans! How often we read of
the lives of great servants of the Lord who have had to
wait years between the conception and birth of a vision.

But his guidance is sure and we need to learn this humility of listening and obeying.

Smith Wigglesworth was sitting at home one day, and suddenly said, 'Let's go to the moor.' His companions had to follow as they made their way up into the hills. On their arrival, Smith spied another man there, went to him, began speaking, and very soon had led him to Jesus. 'We can go home now,' he said. 'We've done what the Lord called us here to do.' And he peremptorily led them all home again.

Myriad tales of such inner guidance fill the pages of the lives of the faithful. Some, however, never quite seem to get it right. I know of those who insist that their every fancy is 'from the Lord', and often will not even listen to the wise advice of their Spirit-led friends, to everyone's pain. Sensitivity to the guidance of the Holy Spirit is more than mere obedience to our inner promptings. We need to filter these through the mesh of Scripture; to remove the dross and leave the pure silver.

Again, do we (will we ever?) fully understand the implications of such a guide living within us? This pillar of fire is no longer before us or behind us, but is now resident. He will tell us what is yet to come. He will 'lift and they will set out'—the Magi were led by the star, a New Testament equivalent of the pillar of fire, being external. I too have had the most amazing experience of God 'going before us'. In a recent visit to Cuba, we went to see many pastors whom we had not met or even contacted beforehand. We discovered that several of them were expecting us! Just two weeks previously one had seen a video of our team's ministry and longed to know more. Another had been advised by the Holy Spirit during a time of prayer, also two weeks previously, that someone from our team would soon contact him. He had never heard of us before! Their response to our visit was enthusiastic, as you can imagine.

Now, however, the Holy Spirit guides us from within as well as from without. Barnabas and Saul were sent on their way by the indwelling Holy Spirit in Acts 13:4 and off they went to Cyprus. He will 'settle' and they will camp, as we later read in Acts 16 of the Spirit of Jesus preventing Paul from entering Bithynia.

That the disciples learned immediately to rely upon this inner guide is evident from the 'committee meeting' in Acts 1. Here they were in deep deliberation over the replacement for Judas Iscariot and the decision was finally decided by casting lots, a traditional method of resolving such decisions throughout the Bible. But it is highly significant that this is the last time that the casting of lots is mentioned in the Bible. After Pentecost, there was no more need of such impersonal arbitration.

Now the Holy Spirit clothed them from on high, and aided their every decision. This is actively recognised in Acts 15:28 when the elders write the decision of the council to the churches with the preface: 'It seemed good to the Holy Spirit and to us. . . .' The council meeting is no less earnest or painstaking than the committee meeting in Acts 1, probably more so, but the whole atmosphere is different. Although Scripture is quoted in both meetings, there is a clarity of thought in the second which is evidently Spirit-inspired. The Holy Fire is the guide.

The important point is, however, that the decision was finally and boldly taken under the guidance of the Holy Spirit by one of the disciples—James in this instance—when he declared: 'It is my judgment, therefore, that we should not make it difficult for the Gentiles who are turning to God' (Acts 15:19). Notice that he declared that it was *his* judgement, but that the others implicitly agreed the rightness of his judgement.

They discussed, but they did not prevaricate. Prevaricators 'whistle among the flocks' with 'much searching of heart', like the leaders of Reuben in Judges 5, when Deborah had called them to war. They were still deep in their theological discussions when it was all over.

Prevarication is not a fruit of the Holy Spirit. It is by no means the same thing as patience. Patience waits upon God's timing or guidance, and when the green light comes on, it moves ahead unhesitatingly and with confidence. Prevarication is trying to decide if the light really is green, and if it is, should we really go ahead?

So in which camp are we? Do we say, 'Here is a move of God, and I am not going to miss out,' and join up with enthusiasm? Or do we call a committee meeting, plan an agenda, develop a programme for debate, investigate the finer points of the way in which God moves, study church history, establish a proper theological foundation (though none of these things are inherently wrong in themselves) and finally maybe, possibly, dip a toe into the water? Is that how Peter got out of the boat when he walked on the water towards Jesus? Did he dangle in a toe first just to test if Jesus' command to come was trustworthy? *No!* He leaped. He landed. He walked. Procrastination is an inability to act in faith. It produces no fruit but doubts.

We have the Counsellor himself within us. But we should not presume that our every whim is God-inspired—we are still much too human and fallible. However, there is a very real sense that if we are in fellowship with the Father, our own decisions, whatever they may be, will be right. Of course the Bible warns us to subject such decisions to the Spirit-led gaze of other mature believers: 'Plans fail for lack of counsel, but with many advisers they succeed' (Prov 15:22).

But Christians are decision-takers. We need never fear for lack of counsel. The Holy Spirit is the best communicator in the world, and he will make clear our paths.

There is a temptation in all of us to prevaricate, especially when faced with life-changing situations, or with the unknown. Decision-making takes faith, and the Holy Spirit amply supplies. Jesus, himself the supreme decision-maker, said: 'But if I do judge, my decisions are right, because I am not alone. I stand with the Father, who sent me' (Jn 8:16).

In the same way, God will bless our decisions because he first guides us by the inner prompting of the Guide, and then trusts us to make them. He doesn't make them for us, for to do so would be to make us his quislings. He loves us too much for that.

The key to walking in faith is to listen and then to act. Listen to the Guide, and obey his lead unhesitatingly. That is faith, and faith produces results. God will never fail to respond to someone walking in faith, for faith pleases him. If we walk in faith God is right there with us, ready to work miracles. It is as though on our left foot is written 'faith', and on our right is written 'fulfilment'. Left, right, left, right, we walk according to his lead.

Freedom and protection

And where the Spirit of the Lord is, there is freedom (2 Cor 3:17).

Indeed, love has often been described as freedom, which it is, and has then been perverted into license, which it is not.

Freedom is the third characteristic of Holy Fire that we identified. We saw how the Holy Fire brought about the freedom of Shadrach, Meshach and Abednego from the fiery furnace, and, more symbolically, the freedom of the Israelites from their slavery. In the passage in 2 Corinthians Paul is talking about the slavery of the deception of the devil. So in this sense freedom and protection go together. Protection from the devil's lies means freedom to understand the truth. The slavery of the sins of pride, bigotry, racism and hatred causes such blindness that people actually believe that by fighting and killing each other, they will gain some kind of advantage. The evil irony is that it is so often carried out in the name of 'freedom'.

But Satan continues to deceive, and with success, even the elect if that were possible, which it is only if we refuse to listen to the Holy Spirit. The Holy Fire of the Spirit of God reveals the truth, and protects his people from the pursuing armies of Satan, standing like a shield as the pillar of fire. When the pillar of fire moved behind God's people who were crossing the Red Sea to protect them, the story tells us that neither the Egyptians nor the Israelites went near each other all night long. When God separates us *to* himself by deeming us to be holy, he separates us *from* the enemy. We are then in the world, but not of the world.

It is not just the lies of Satan which are rendered powerless. For when Balaam tried to curse Israel and instead prophesied: 'There is no sorcery against Jacob, no divination against Israel' (Num 23:23), the powerlessness of Satan when confronted with the power of God was manifest. Proverbs puts it more graphically: 'Like a fluttering sparrow or a darting swallow, an undeserved curse does not come to rest' (Prov 26:2).

Reinhard Bonnke tells of an incident which happened during one of his gospel crusades in Africa, when a famous witch from the United States was invited by other local witches to come and curse the preacher on the platform, because they had tried and their curses weren't working. She duly arrived and tried her strongest brew of curses, but they merely rebounded upon herself. She went home in disgrace. We know about this, because one of the inviting witches was honest enough to admit his impotence against the protection of the Holy Spirit, and gave his life to Jesus!

In 2 Kings 6 we see Elisha with his servant facing the strong Aramean army. At his servant's dismay, Elisha prays to the Lord that the eyes of his servant will be opened, and he sees 'horses and chariots of fire all round Elisha'. Surely the One who is in us is greater than the one who is in the world!

It is false doctrine to teach that if we are walking with God then trouble will never happen to us. God himself permits trouble, as we shall see in the next chapter. But under the protection of the Holy Spirit Satan can do nothing. Should he try, he would be instantly consumed by the Holy Fire who dwells within us. Though he knows his end, he has no wish to hasten it. That is the extent of our protection! No wonder his fiery darts cannot penetrate our shield of faith—like a meteorite entering the earth's atmosphere at high speed, they are burned up by the protective shield of the Holy Fire of God as they approach!

It has also been well said that flies do not settle on a hot stove. Demons are not comfortable in the presence of the Holy Spirit who is a consuming fire. Where the Holy Spirit dwells, no evil creature can survive. This is why it is impossible for a Christian to be demon-possessed. Both the Holy Spirit and the demon would have to dwell together—that is, occupy the spirit of the believer—which would mean instant destruction for the demon. But his time for that will come later, and he must leave immediately when confronted with the power of the Holy Spirit.

Though it is clear from this argument that a Christian cannot be possessed by a demon—that is, for the demon to possess the *spirit* of the person—many believe that it is possible for a Christian to be oppressed by a demon within an area of his *soul*. This, however, then begs the question as to whether we can be partially saved in our souls. Obviously not, as we have already discussed. Partial salvation is no salvation at all. The Holy Fire of God would destroy the unholy, and we would be consumed.

Then where does this leave the poor Christian who clearly manifests a demonic presence? Do we say that they were never saved in the first place? That seems unfair and unlikely. Or was their manifestation simply a deception of the devil to confuse us all? If so, how can he have the 'right' to so humiliate a believer? And how does it gain the devil when so many are set free and their lives are totally changed? I believe that the answer, like so much of Scripture, is actually very simple.

We know that even after we become believers we still do not submit to God control over every area of our lives. We still sin, even though we don't want to. Paul describes this conflict graphically in Romans 7. But we are not consumed, due to the graciousness of God, who has proclaimed us to be holy through Jesus. So our continuing sinfulness is removed by a loving God, provided that we continually seek him. I am saved, but I still have some vile habits. Though I am a Christian, washed by the blood of Jesus, I am not immune to pride, conceit or harbouring evil thoughts, since God allows me free will, and I struggle just as Paul did. How often we are grateful to God for revealing a dirty area of our soulish life that needs to be dealt with, and how grateful also are we that he doesn't reveal those wrong areas all at once! Like a wax candle we would crumple under the heat of his perfection. Many of our evil ways we are therefore unaware of until the spotlight of the Holy Spirit reveals them to us. This means that although we are saved, we continue to harbour sinful areas, often unwittingly. Therefore I believe that it is perfectly possible that some of these areas have a demonic influence, or origin.

The Holy Fire of the Holy Spirit would consume any demon who tried to possess his territory, but God in his mercy allows our still-tainted souls to come to a slow cleansing. *If he were to deal instantly with all the dirt that still influences our souls, he would damage us also, because consciously or unconsciously we are still holding on to it.* God is far more patient than we can understand, and will deal with each area of our lives as and when he reveals the needs and we submit that area to him. This is why we must submit to God before we resist the devil (Jas 4:7), and *then* the devil will flee from us.

This should not, however, give us a conviction that we may all still harbour demons. I am not of the school of thought that declares that we should all go through prolonged exorcisms just to make sure! We do not need to hunt for 'reds under the beds'. The Holy Spirit does it far more effectively than we ever can, and we need to put our faith in his protection, not in our own efforts. In fact I am convinced that in the vast majority of cases, when the Holy Spirit moves in, Satan moves out comprehensively, taking all his minions with him.

If a demon does manifest itself, then let us stamp on it and get on with our lives. We are not called to gleefully hunt for demons in great orgies of deliverance, but to cast them out if and when they make an appearance. In fact Jesus specifically commanded us *not* to rejoice that the demons submit to us (Lk 10:20), precisely so that we should not get this matter out of perspective.

We shall look at the principles behind this in rather more detail in the next chapter, when we come to consider purification.

Power

When Jesus promised the Holy Spirit, he promised power. When the Holy Spirit came upon the chosen few in the Old Testament, he came in power. The disciples were in absolutely no doubt when the Holy Spirit came at Pentecost that this was what Jesus had been talking about and promising all along, and that they now had that power. There was no need to ask for it any further. Indeed, they never did again. They knew that the power of the Holy Spirit was now with them. They were refilled on later occasions, but no longer needed to ask for power. Rather they sought the source of the power instead.

Let us be conscious of the implications. The Holy Fire of which we have been reading now lives within each born-again believer, the more demonstrably so in those baptised in the Holy Spirit. Can we glibly continue our lives as though nothing has happened? That same power which created the universe; that same fire which breathed life into Adam; that same which destroyed the soldiers at the furnace; that incomparably great power which God exerted in Christ when he raised him from the dead; *that* Holy Fire now lives within the four walls of this feeble flesh. 'Don't you know that you yourselves are God's temple and that God's Spirit lives in you?' (1 Cor 3:16).

Let us not become confused into thinking that the baptism of the Holy Spirit empowers us to heal the sick, to drive out demons and to preach the gospel. These things the disciples did long before Pentecost. For the Holy Spirit makes his home in *every* believer, and it is every Christian's duty and ability to do these things whether or not they have been baptised in the Holy Spirit. No, the baptism remains God's covenant sign, but there is power in that sign. Jesus describes the coming of the sign in terms of being 'clothed' (Lk 24:49). Clothing wraps around the outside of the body, keeping it warm, keeping it modest, keeping it clean, keeping it protected, keeping it attractive. Clothing reflects our personality. But the Holy Spirit does much more than just look after the body of the individual. He similarly looks after the whole body of Christ.

The fruits of the Spirit described in Galatians 5:22 are produced by the inner working of the Holy Spirit upon an individual soul, through his indwelling, which occurs when we are saved. The gifts of the Holy Spirit are outward manifestations of the power of the Holy Spirit in the lives of believers who have been baptised in the Holy Spirit, by the outworking of that Spirit, in order to build up the whole body of Christ, by mutual encouragement, support and edification. The one comes to us by being the home of the Holy Spirit; the other from being clothed by the same Spirit. The one is internal, the other external. The one is a presence, the other a sign both to believers and to unbelievers alike.

The outward manifestations of the power of the Holy Fire of the Holy Spirit have from the beginning caused both fear and conviction. When chasing the Israelites through the Red Sea, the Egyptians shouted: 'Let's get away from the Israelites! The Lord is fighting for them against Egypt' (Exod 14:25).

Nebuchadnezzar immediately erupted into unfamiliar praise of God when his victims emerged unscathed from the fiery furnace. 'Praise be to God,' he cried, adding, 'for no other God can save in this way' (Dan 3:28–29). He was converted by a manifestation of the power of the Holy Spirit. How clearly Paul saw this too when he wrote to the Corinthians: 'My message and my preaching were not with wise and persuasive words, but with a demonstration of the Spirit's power, so that your faith might not rest on men's wisdom, but on God's power' (1 Cor 2:4–5).

This power is awesome, as we have seen, and not to be trifled with. *Just because God as the Holy Spirit now dwells within us, that doesn't diminish his awesome holiness.* Ananias and Sapphira made the mistake of underestimating this holy power in just the same way as Uzzah did. It is still happening today.

Being aware of his presence and his holiness should make us very much more conscious of our need to be holy, 'even as our Father in heaven is holy'. We should never make light of his indwelling. Many believers today are very casual about the holy nature of the God who lives within them. Paul said that it was for this reason that some had fallen asleep, for they had eaten and drunk judgement upon themselves, treating irreverently the holy sacrament of the Lord. He was speaking of the Lord's Supper, but the principle remains the same. Within me is the power of God. It is instantly destructive to the unholy. It is only by the grace of God that I am what I am, declared to be holy by faith in the power of the blood in his Son, Jesus. How dare I be disrespectful of such power? How dare I take such a fearsome risk? What a merciful God I have, that I live at all!

All across the globe today, from Toronto to Timbuktu, there is a new outpouring of God's fire. Millions are literally feeling the touch of God in amazing manifestations. They are being empowered by the Holy Spirit in a new way to go into all the world and preach the good news. It is instructive to note that almost all the manifestations of the Holy Spirit being seen today have been described exactly in previous revivals, and indeed are predicted in the Bible as evidence of the outpouring of the Spirit.

However, there is in mankind that which would seek the bread rather than the giver of that bread. After the feeding of the five thousand, the crowds sought out Jesus to ask

him to give them further miraculous signs—ie, more bread
for themselves. But Jesus said, 'I am the bread of life' (Jn
6:35).

As believers we are not immune to falling into the same
trap. If Satan cannot prevent us from receiving the power
of the Holy Spirit, he will try to so distort the effects that
others are persuaded not to participate. So we see some
who seek the manifestations rather than the Holy Spirit,
just like the crowds sought after Jesus. Others, perhaps not
fully understanding what is going on, begin to pervert the
cause of the Spirit by fleshly imitation or uncontrolled
excess. These exhibitions then bring many to doubt and
to fear what the Spirit is doing, attracting attention to the
manifestations instead of to the inner working of the Holy
Spirit and the fruits of these renewed lives.

It is partly for this reason that I have felt constrained to
write this book. Let us remember that the Holy Spirit is
first and foremost a *holy* Spirit. Let us seek him with all
our heart, and when we come under his power and his
anointing, even if that means odd manifestations if that is
what he wants to do, let us rejoice and glory in him. But
let us use what he gives us for his glory. Let us go forth
and preach the good news to the poor, bind up the broken-
hearted and proclaim freedom for the captives and release
from darkness for the prisoners. Let us spread this wonderful power around the world so that the whole world may
hear and know and see that Jesus is Lord!

Let us by all means come to him for refreshment and
empowering, but after we have been refreshed, after we
have drunk from the river of life, let us not continue to
gather merely to revel in the manifestations of his power.
It is like a photographer spending all his life showing off
his new camera without ever taking a picture. I have no
problem with manifestations. I do have a problem with

those who seek them for their own sake. That cannot and will not glorify God. God's power is for God's purpose.

Let it also be said here, however, that the majority of the revivals of history have been halted after only a few years because church leaders have denigrated the whole movement through the emotionalism of some of the participants and quenched the Spirit. We have been guilty of throwing out the baby with the bathwater. Dear God, forgive us.

Let us pray earnestly that this time we can, by the grace of God, be mature enough to learn to handle this astonishing gift of his Holy Fire. May the enthusiasts be so filled with his power that their fruit is sufficient testimony to God's power. Indeed may we all become enthusiasts, for the word actually means 'to be filled with God'. May the leaders be wise in discernment and hesitant to be critical of what God is doing, restricting their criticism, correctly, for the few who pervert the cause by misuse.

Our God is holy, and we must all remember that. If we rebel, we shall be consumed. How much more if we are already filled with the Holy Spirit:

> It is impossible for those who have once been enlightened, who have tasted the heavenly gift, who have shared in the Holy Spirit, who have tasted the goodness of the word of God and the powers of the coming age, if they fall away, to be brought back to repentance, because to their loss they are crucifying the Son of God all over again and subjecting him to public disgrace (Heb 6:4–6).

Then surely we fall into the hands of the living God, who is a consuming fire. If we rebel, we self-destruct.

Motivation

In these last days God is pouring out his Holy Spirit. There is a new life and zeal in the church. But this power has not

suddenly changed; thankfully his presence changes us. It is
we who are suddenly motivated where before we were not.

We saw in the furnace how Shadrach, Meshach and
Abednego did not merely sit around warming themselves
in the delightful presence of the fire of God, but were
active, walking around with him. The Holy Spirit is a
motivator. When he came at Pentecost, the disciples
acted at once. After all, the book is called 'Acts'! Gone
were the dreary committee meetings to decide who should
do what. Now salvation was uppermost in their minds.
The same happens today. *Whenever the Holy Spirit
clothes us in the same way, God's priorities drench our
soul.* Before, we knew that people should be saved. Now
we feel that need deeply with all the urgency of God's
Spirit driving us on to effective witness. Before, we
rejoiced when people were healed or delivered. Now we
long to be involved. It was the boldness of the disciples
that caused the rulers to take note that they had been with
Jesus, not their status or scholarship.

Motivation and power go together. The power of faith is
only released by action, and action by motivation. If we
are not motivated, nothing happens, regardless of how
gifted we may be. The unmotivated concert pianist gives
few concerts. In my old school, the fastest runner among
us ran like a stag! When he ran, no one could touch him.
But he hated running, so he very rarely, if ever, competed.
As a result, the second fastest won all the prizes. That
second fastest man later went on to become an Olympic
medalist in the Mexico Olympics. I never heard of the
faster one again. Without motivation, all gifts are wasted.

With the clothing of the Holy Spirit, all that changes.
Instead, with Paul, we find divine motivation: 'Yet when I
preach the gospel, I cannot boast, for I am compelled to
preach. Woe to me if I do not preach the gospel!' (1 Cor
9:16).

An inner drive to be about the Father's business is the hallmark of the Holy Fire of God upon the lives of the saints.

Recognition and identification

When the Holy Spirit fell upon the disciples at Pentecost, not only did their whole lives change, but the attitude of the people and the authorities towards them changed.

Until then it could be said that they were, if not exactly in hiding, then at least being careful not to advertise their existence too openly; not to upset the status quo. They were a small band of dedicated followers, quietly minding their own business. And the locals, even if they did know of their activities, were content that they were not imposing their views upon the rest, and that they should continue to have their strange beliefs if that was what they wanted to do. 'You do your thing and let me do mine' was the prevalent attitude. What a picture this is of the attitude of secular society to the church today, which is in itself a sad reflection upon the general lack of a demonstration of the power of the Holy Fire.

That situation could have trickled on for years. But then an explosion of God's power changed everything. The reaction of the people to Pentecost was immediate: people were bewildered, utterly amazed and perplexed. Large crowds gathered out of curiosity. Some mocked the disciples as being drunk, but then the preaching 'cut to the heart' (Acts 2:37) and they repented. Later we read that everyone was filled with awe, and the disciples were 'enjoying the favour of all the people' (Acts 2:47).

When the power of the Holy Spirit is moving, it is inherently attractive, not just to believers but to unbelievers as well. The ministry of Jesus himself demonstrates the same thing. He said about the Spirit: 'When he comes, he

will convict the world of guilt in regard to sin and righteousness and judgment' (Jn 16:8). He will make an impact
on the world, and the world will recognise those through
whom he comes. Thousands crowded to Jesus out of curiosity because they recognised power and authority when
they saw it, were humble enough to admit their need, and
wanted to partake of this heavenly feast. What they saw was
attractive and they wanted in.

Today is no different. There are millions who, when
they see the power of the Holy Spirit at work, immediately
want to be part of it—to experience the power for themselves. And when that power is released, things happen!
Thank God for his wonderful outpouring across many
nations today. Without finding fault or favour, God is
blessing his people with his power. That power manifested in the lives of the believers changes the percep-
tions of those outside the church. It is impossible to be
indifferent when things are happening which are evidently
supernatural. The great secularists of the twentieth century
are challenged into responding. So many thousands of
healings cannot all be flagrant hoaxes. He touches people's bodies. So many thousands of people rejoicing or
laughing or crying under the anointing power of the Spirit
cannot be denied. He touches people's hearts. So many
thousands prepared to lay down their lives for the love of
Jesus cannot be ignored. He touches people's wills.

While there may be gentle mockery of some of the
stranger manifestations, and indeed we can laugh at
ourselves sometimes too, it is significant that today's
media, so gloatingly hostile to the smallest whiff of
hypocrisy, have been more hesitant to dismiss the new
move of God's fire in the lives of believers. Only those
with vested power interests, the religious and secular
authorities, respond antagonistically, just as they did in
the days of Jesus' ministry. Why? Because their power

bases are threatened by something, or rather by Some-one, whom they instinctively recognise as having the power to topple their ivory towers. So it is that the greatest vilification of those moving in the anointing power of the Holy Spirit comes from the leadership of the dead religious institutions. How little has changed in 2,000 years!

Pride can't abide humility. So the reaction of the Jewish leaders was totally different from that of the general public. We read that they were 'greatly disturbed' (Acts 4:2), although they were astonished by the courage of the disciples. But they began to threaten and systematically persecute them in their attempts to destroy the work of the Spirit. No such persecution of the disciples took place before Pentecost.

Today we see the same response. Whenever the Spirit is moving, thousands flock to soak in his goodness, their lives transformed by his power, while others rise up in protest. The Holy Fire is a separating fire. So the coming of the Holy Fire brings two types of recognition. On the one hand, people are inherently attracted and acknowledge that the power of God rests upon those so blessed; on the other, there are those who recognise the threat to their position and respond accordingly. It is often said that 'the Spirit divides'. Others say that 'the Spirit unites'. Both are true. But when he comes, none can be indifferent!

Discriminatory power

The final characteristic that we identified as belonging to the Holy Fire of God was the power to discriminate between the holy and the unholy. This has already been discussed in some detail in this chapter, but this aspect of the Holy Fire is such an inherent part of God's nature, and so fundamental to the whole tenor of Scripture, that we need to see if we can discover a little more of how this fire works in our lives.

We have seen how Holy Fire destroys the unholy but edifies the holy. Until now, the implication has been that the person is treated as a whole—that is, either wholly holy or wholly unholy—and responds to the presence of the Holy Fire accordingly. But this needs to be qualified. Are all unbelievers wholly unholy? And are all believers completely holy? If the answers to these questions are 'no' (and we know that they are), then in what way do we see them reacting to the Holy Fire? If all sin brings instant destruction, why does Jesus speak of greater and lesser sins? John 19:11 says, 'Jesus answered, ''You would have no power over me if it were not given to you from above. Therefore the one who handed me over to you is guilty of a greater sin.'' ' Surely people cannot be more destroyed or less destroyed? It doesn't seem to make sense.

But God has a better plan, and more compassion. Let us see what we can find out by looking at the purifying fire.

7

Purifying Fire

There is a theme which runs through Scripture like blood through a vein. It courses from the heartbeat of God to the extremities of his creation. It is the secret of health, and the foundation upon which the whole design of nature runs. Like oil, it lubricates and liberates the work of his hands to perfection. It is the theme of cleanliness.

Unnatural entropy

Cleanliness implies separation, which in turn implies differentiation. The laws of thermodynamics tell us that, left to time, chance and their own devices, all things will eventually disorganise into an evenly distributed mishmash of formless matter and energy—a process known as entropy. Even the hard-working housewife, sweeping each day's dust from her doorway knows that, without the scientists having to produce mathematical formulae to convince her! But how and why is this?

The created world around us is anything but a mishmash, and therefore anything but chance. There is such diversity that the hand of the Creator is clearly seen, his character perfectly reflected in what he has made.

As soon as unintended matter begins to get in the door, imperfection creeps in with it and perfection begins to deteriorate. Dirt, damage, decline, disease, decay and

death follow as night follows day. In the perfect hands of
the Creator such a thing would be impossible and even
unthinkable. There has to be another hand and another
design behind it.

After the creation, there had to be an initiation of this
process of decline, which could not have come from God.
So it is that the Fall explains the imperfect world we see.
Man's deliberate decision to disobey God, having been
given the freewill in order to love him, uses that freewill
instead to assert his own independence. That first sin put a
very real spanner in the perfect works of all creation, and
led to the beginning of the degeneration of all matter.
Creation has groaned ever since.

Yet it is not enough just to state that left to itself
everything will degenerate, and to leave it at that. If
God's purpose had not been interfered with, nothing
would degenerate from the pattern that he created. The
force of entropy is therefore an actively destructive force,
not a passive one. It destroys the works that God has
made, and even though it would seem to be a 'natural'
force, it is again unthinkable that God would invent a
universe that naturally fights against his intended for-
mat! Entropy is therefore a consequence of sin, and seen
in that light it brings the enormity of it into stark reality.
Satan is the destroyer, the lord of entropy! Man is his
colluder.

This is the fundamental basis for the story of creation,
and why the popular theory of evolution denies not only
the written word of God, but also the principle of sin. A
sin-filled world is not merely a degenerate world. It is a
degenerating world, not a regenerating one. Evolutionists
(and New Agers) would have us believe that the world of
today, by a process of mutation and development of new
kinds, becomes better adjusted to the environment day by
day; that everything is getting better (and presumably will

one day be perfect). The creation story, on the other hand, tells us that everything was once perfect and is now in decline through sin.

The two concepts are irreconcilably opposed. They are two trains going in opposite directions—one downhill and the other up. You cannot have your cake and eat it. The world we see, and the one the scientists measure, is clearly degenerating.

So how is this relevant to the idea of cleanliness? Someone once defined a weed as 'a plant in the wrong place'. Similarly, dirt is matter in the wrong place. Its presence is imperfection, a symbol of the decline of God's creation through the sin of man. Cleanliness becomes therefore more than just a counter-symbol, but a real attempt to put the clock back—to *restore* the originally intended differentiation and distinction of God's design. It is a fight against those laws of thermo-dynamics!

Heavenly restoration

It is no surprise that when God instituted the original law through Moses its main emphasis was upon purity. The importance of cleanliness in the early Jewish ritual cannot be overstated. Whole pages of the Pentateuch are devoted to it in almost obsessional detail. One-third of the book of Leviticus alone deals exclusively with this subject, and that doesn't include any concern with moral cleansing. Ritual washing; ceremonial cleanliness; sacrifices; sprinkling with blood and with water of cleansing; shaving bodies; washing hands and feet; washing and changing clothes; cedarwood, scarlet wool and hyssop; clean and unclean animals; clean and unclean foods; purgings of mildews and diseases; bodily excretions; flows of blood; contact with dead bodies; the list is almost endless, and it pervades Scripture. God is obviously concerned about being—and keeping—clean!

Cleanliness is therefore a restoration of God's purpose. It is a re-establishment of his intended form. It is the spiritual pull towards God and away from entropy—heavenly restoration. Therefore those of us who are concerned to follow God's law, who are filled with his Spirit, who strive to be more like him, will consequently have deep within us that Spirit-inspired urge for cleanliness. This is first manifested in a desire to be done with our inherent sinfulness, but as the Spirit does his work, we become more aware of other aspects of uncleanness in our lives.

The Dani tribe of Indonesia were once one of the headhunter tribes of Irian Jaya—the island of which Papua New Guinea is the other half. Their culture was dominated by the worship of evil spirits. They wore no clothes except a gourd, and lived in filthy conditions, often defecating on their own doorsteps. They rarely washed, and the men wore their hair in huge filthy pigtails, in which was supposed to reside their strength.

A Christian missionary visited them and worked with them for many months, bringing these naked tribesfolk improved medicines and diet. When he had learned some of their language he shared the good news of Jesus with them. After some months, many had accepted the gospel and received Jesus as their Lord and Saviour.

The missionary had deliberately and carefully refrained from teaching any Western culture, avoiding even the teaching of songs. But not long after these primitive people had become Christians, they began spontaneously to wash, and dress, and cut their hair for the very first time in the history of their tribe. No one had suggested they should do so, except the Holy Spirit. The missionary even questioned their motives, and was told that the Spirit had told them, and they wanted to obey him.

Here is the purifying fire at work in simplest form: convicting, cleansing, restoring. We shall return to his methods a little later in this chapter. It is not my purpose here to study at great depth the spiritual or historical significance of all the various Mosaic laws regarding purification. Besides, I do not pretend to know or understand a fraction of why cedarwood or scarlet wool should have been used, for example. So let me leave what I know little of, and return to fire and some basic principles.

Principles of purification

From that admittedly rather philosophical introduction, we have established that purification is a process of restoration.

This process requires three conditions.

1. That there is a mixture of good and bad; clean and dirty

We discovered that sin brought this about, and that entropy results. In a perfect world no purification is necessary, since there is nothing to remove. There will be no purification in heaven!

2. That they can be separated, ie, respond differently to an outside input or action

A broom is designed to move the dirt and not the floor. If the detergent were to dissolve the clothes as well as the grease, no cleansing would happen, only destruction. *There must be a discriminating force.* For example, we see provision made in Numbers 31:23 for whatever could not stand fire, which should instead be purified with water. Since the fire would burn everything there would be no discrimination.

3. That having been separated the dirty can be collected and discarded or destroyed

It must not be so intricately united with the clean that the removal destroys the clean. Jesus knew this when he told the parable of the weeds in Matthew 13. The owner said, 'While you are pulling the weeds, you may root up the wheat with them' (Mt 13:29). Later, the weeds were to be pulled up, tied into bundles (dealt with unceremoniously) and burned.

Each summer we see monstrous combine harvesters munching across our cornfields, gathering in next year's food supply. The whole plant—stem, leaves, ear and grain—is cut from the stubble, and passed into the threshing drum, where a maelstrom awaits it. Here a massive spinning cage smashes the plant into a thousand pieces. This mixture is then passed over a series of sieves and fans, which separate the good grain into the tank, while the chaff, straw and dust are belched from the rear of the huge machine. We see a mixture separated and the rubbish discarded.

Only if all these conditions pertain can cleansing, or purification, take place. These then are the necessary precursors for the process, so how does God go about it?

Blood and fire

As we have seen, the Bible is full of methods of purification, from sacrifice, to washing, to sprinkling with blood. But the two most important elements are blood and fire. Often these two would work in tandem, for example in the Mosaic sacrifices, when an animal was killed, its blood was sprinkled on the altar, and then it was burned on the fire. Death and destruction; blood and fire. As we have already seen, these are substitutes for sin, so that the people may enjoy their counterparts: life and restoration; or as we now see: life and purification.

So there are not just two elements, blood and fire, but also two purposes, life and purification. They are not always the same thing, as we shall discover in this chapter.

Without blood there is no forgiveness. Hebrews 9:22 tells us: 'In fact, the law requires that nearly everything be cleansed with blood, and without the shedding of blood there is no forgiveness.' Without forgiveness there is no salvation, and the chapter goes on to explain that Jesus died once for all to do away with sin. This sin is no longer merely atoned for, which means covered over, but done away with. The blood of goats and bulls only atones for, or covers over, sin. But the blood of Christ takes it away. So verse 22 above is referring to this act of cleansing—the removal of inherent sin, leading to salvation. Why this is important we shall soon see.

So first must come the blood, then comes the fire. In just the same way that salvation must come before the baptism of the Holy Spirit, so the cleansing blood comes before the purifying fire. Again, at Pentecost (Acts 2:19) Peter quotes Joel's 'blood and fire and billows of smoke'. That is the divine order: salvation, Holy Spirit and glory!

But what is so special about fire that it purifies?

First, we need something which will separate. We have already seen that Holy Fire is not just a separate fire, but a separating fire. Fire is recognised as being the most purifying force that exists—with the greatest power of differentiation. This is graphically described by Ezekiel in chapter 24 when describing the judgement about to befall Jerusalem:

Therefore this is what the Sovereign Lord says: 'Woe to the city of bloodshed! I, too, will pile the wood high. So heap on the wood and kindle the fire. Cook the meat well, mixing in the spices; and let the bones be charred. Then set the empty pot on the coals till it becomes hot and its copper glows so its impurities may be melted and its deposit burned away. It has frustrated *all* efforts; its heavy deposit has not been removed, *not even by fire*. Now your impurity is lewdness. Because I tried to cleanse you but you would not be cleansed from your impurity, you will not be clean again until my wrath against you has subsided' (Ezek 24:9–13, my emphasis).

Through his prophet, God is grieving over his people's hardness, their inability to respond to the process of purification, even by fire. It is clear from the context that fire was the greatest of all efforts. The normal process of cooking is a purifying one, destroying bacteria and often some poisons. God is saying here that the normal processes of purifying his people have failed. So more heat is applied, until the food is burned up. Still no cleansing, so now he turns up the heat until even the pot itself is melted—*still* without result!

Now the hottest fires known in the days of the Old Testament were those which were used to melt and refine metal, during which the unmelted impurities would float to the surface of the glowing liquid to form the dross which would be scraped away, leaving the pure molten metal beneath. In the purifying, this process would be repeated several times until no more dross formed. 'And the words of the Lord are flawless, like silver refined in a furnace of clay, purified seven times' (Ps 12:6).

Sometimes, unwanted metals such as lead could be removed from gold or silver in this way, and again the Bible uses these pictures to illustrate God's attempts to purify his people with all the power at his command: 'The bellows blow fiercely to burn away the lead with fire, but the refining goes on in vain; the wicked are not purged out' (Jer 6:29). The prophet is decrying the fact that the pure and the impure are too intricately interwoven to be separated, even by fire. So no purification can take place, just as Ezekiel had prophesied.

These are more than mere pictures. God intends to purify with real fire—with Holy Fire. Holy Fire discriminates; separates the holy from the unholy. And despite God's frustrated attempts with his hard and rebellious house Israel, he fully intends to continue the process with those who will respond: 'This third I will bring into the fire; I will refine them like silver and test them like gold. They will call on my name and I will answer them; I will say, ''They are my people,'' and they will say, ''The Lord is our God'' ' (Zech 13:9).

This is a glorious 'remnant' promise that though not all will turn back to the Lord, some will. And this fire is not just some form of testing through suffering on this earth, or his judgement carried out by a worldly king, but is the very presence of the Lord himself: 'But who can endure the day of his coming? Who can stand when he appears? For he will be like a refiner's fire or a launderer's soap' (Mal 3:2). The Lord himself is the refining fire that will appear and separate on the day of his coming.

Paul describes the same scene in 1 Corinthians 3:

If any man builds on this foundation using gold, silver, costly stones, wood, hay or straw, his work will be shown for what it is, because the Day will bring it to light. It will be revealed with fire, and the fire will test the quality of each man's work. If what he has built survives, he will receive his reward. If it is burned up, he will suffer loss; he himself will be saved, but only as one escaping through the flames (vv. 12–15).

There is much more to this scripture than simply the refining (or testing) of the child of God and his work, but we will return to it in a later chapter. For the

moment, it is sufficient to note the separating purification
of the Holy Fire.

Secondly, fire does more than separate; it also destroys,
as we see from the above scriptures. So it completes the
full process of purification in one fell swoop. The rubbish
is both separated *and* destroyed. Again this is characteristic of Holy Fire, destroying the unholy but leaving the
holy. This is why it is such a powerful force.

We have seen how this process can apply to nations and
to peoples. Unholy individuals can be weeded out and
destroyed. Even unholy nations can be brought down.
But what happens within the life of a believer? How can
and does the Holy Fire operate? Am I instantly purified
when I am saved? Or when I receive the baptism of the
Holy Spirit? If so, and I am deemed holy (and therefore
perfect) in the sight of God, how is it that I continue to
sin?

The paradox of sin

Here is an underlying paradox which has troubled believers since before John wrote his first letter, and needs to be
sorted out before we can progress to discover how the
purifying fire of God actually works. So let us take what at
first appears to be a small diversion from our journey of
discovery, but which will prove illuminating.

The paradox is this: If I am a Christian, I am born again.
I am a new creature. The Holy Spirit lives within me. And
yet I still sin. I do not want to, but I find myself sinning.
Paul beautifully describes the internal tussle in Romans 7.
But John says in his first letter that if I continue to sin, I
am not born of God: 'No-one who is born of God will
continue to sin, because God's seed remains in him; he
cannot go on sinning, because he has been born of God' (1
Jn 3:9). This seems to imply that I am not a Christian after

all! So am I or aren't I? What is my true situation? 'What a wretched man I am!' says Paul (Rom 7:24). This is the poser.

But John, at the beginning of this same letter, writes: 'If we claim to be without sin, we deceive ourselves and the truth is not in us. If we confess our sins, he is faithful and just and will forgive us our sins and purify us from all unrighteousness' (1 Jn 1:8–9). Let us remember that John is writing to *believers*, not to unbelievers, and therefore he is expecting believers to sin, and not only to sin, but to confess their sins. How then can he write only a chapter or two later that no one who is born of God will continue to sin, when he has just said we should confess our sins?

I believe that the secret to this paradox is hidden within the verse just quoted above, where John says that God will forgive us our sins *and* purify us from all unrighteousness. He is not merely repeating words for their own sake, but clearly means that two distinct processes are taking place—forgiveness and purification. Or to put it in longer words, justification and sanctification.

A year or two ago, God gave me a new understanding about a well-known passage of Scripture which has helped me to appreciate what is happening, and how great is the loving-kindness of our forgiving God.

Clean body, dirty feet

In John 13, during the Last Supper, Jesus gets up, takes off his robe, wraps a towel around his waist and begins to wash the feet of the disciples. While he is going from disciple to disciple, there must have been a look of pure horror on Peter's face. How could his Lord and Master so demean himself as to perform this base task—the job of the humblest slave? Besides, had they not already had their feet washed when they came in? He knew Jesus did some odd things, but this was not just odd, it was obscene! So when Jesus comes to Peter, an interesting and strangely revealing conversation takes place:

> He came to Simon Peter, who said to him, 'Lord, are you going to wash my feet?'
> Jesus replied, 'You do not realise now what I am doing, but later you will understand.'
> 'No,' said Peter, 'you shall never wash my feet.'
> Jesus answered, 'Unless I wash you, you have no part with me.'
> 'Then, Lord,' Simon Peter replied, 'not just my feet but my hands and my head as well!'
> Jesus answered, 'A person who has had a bath needs only to wash his feet; his whole body is clean. And you are clean, though not every one of you.' For he knew who was going to betray him, and that was why he said not every one was clean (Jn 13:6–11).

Now we all know that this passage is about humility and serving one another—humbling ourselves before one another—for whoever wants to be first must be the servant of all. That is undoubtedly true. But suddenly I saw that it is about something else as well, perhaps even more fundamental. I saw that the whole passage is also about *forgiveness*. It tells us about the one-off event of justification and the subsequent process of sanctification. How is this?

Jesus said to Peter that unless he washed him he could have no part with him. We need to understand that in the Lord's day foot-washing was a regular daily, or even more frequent, occurrence, usually whenever a guest entered a house. Bathing was not as regular as it would be in Western society today.

Now justification is our reconciliation with our heavenly Father, brought about by the death of Jesus, who died first of all in order to deal with the Adam-nature of man, the inherited sinfulness about which we can do nothing. Jesus died that mankind—the one who receives him by faith—should have a solution to his fundamentally wrong nature. Then he also died that the past sins may be forgiven; that is, the baggage of sin which each individual brings with him when he comes to Jesus—his sin history—the accumulated dirt of his life. We are indeed made into a totally new creation, washed clean both on the inside and the outside. We are totally different inside and out.

But we cannot come to Jesus today for tomorrow's sin! Otherwise I could be forgiven now for all the sins of the future, and live the life of Riley from now on! Paul justly condemns such an attitude: 'What then? Shall we sin because we are not under law but under grace? By no means!' (Rom 6:15). Therefore there needs to be a regular 'updating' of our cleansing, if and when we fall.

Which brings us to sanctification. This regular cleansing is the day-by-day process of chipping away at our fleshly nature, which is constantly at war with the Spirit. It is the breaking down of our 'self' to allow the Spirit to grow within us. It happens through a constant process of submission to the will of God, of allowing God to deal with issues, habits, thoughts and fears—and sins—which continue to beset us after our salvation. No one becomes instantly like Jesus!

Let me use the illustration of an egg. If the yolk represents the spirit, the white the soul and the shell the body, then before we are saved it is as though we are an unfertilised egg. On the outside it may not look wrong, but inside the yolk there is no life. However much care is taken, all it will do eventually is rot. Now when we are saved it is as though God breathes life into the yolk by his Spirit, and it becomes fertilised. That is the moment of justification. Now it is totally different, although to begin with only one cell is! Now there is life there, and if properly incubated that life will grow, consuming the white bit by bit until finally the chick chips its way out of the shell. That is the process of sanctification.

Now let us look at the passage in John 13 again. Jesus tells Peter: 'A person who has had a bath needs only to wash his feet; his whole body is clean.' Here there are two things happening—bathing and foot-washing. Both appear to be totally necessary, and cannot replace each other. They signify our general cleansing (that is, our justification), and our specific regular cleansing (that is, our sanctification). First we need to have a bath—that is, to be saved. After that we need to have our feet washed— that is, to be cleansed daily.

Why feet? Why not hands and head as well, as Peter suggested? I asked the Lord the same question, and this is what he told me: *The feet are the one part of us which is constantly in touch with the earth—with the dirt of this world!* However clean we may be, whenever we walk in this world (even though we are in the world and not of the world) we will become contaminated by the dirt of this world, because there is that within our nature—our fleshly nature—which is sticky and picks up dirt.

It is as though we are like pieces of coal before we are saved. Coal is black, and if a knob of coal is broken in half, it is black throughout. That is a picture of our state before we come to Christ. When we are saved, it is as though God changes us into a piece of marble, white all the way through. There is a fundamental change of nature. But if that piece of marble were to be thrown into a coal scuttle, it would not be long before it would begin to look like a piece of coal again. Of course if you broke it open you would see the difference. It would be white on the inside, but black on the outside. That is the state of the Christian who is not sanctified. But take it from the coal scuttle and wash it under the tap, and soon the difference is easily seen again.

Of course there is another type—that is white-painted coal! These are the hypocrites, the white-washed tombs that Jesus castigated so roundly. Washing *them* only shows up their real nature, black inside, which is why they were so unhappy to be exposed by Jesus. A hypocrite never wants to be washed by Jesus. Indeed, Jesus knew which one among his disciples fell into this category when he pointed out that not every one was clean. It is highly significant that immediately after Jesus washed Judas' feet, he went out and betrayed him—his true nature being revealed.

So we conclude then that Jesus was teaching his disciples that they needed first to be saved (justified), that is to 'have a bath'; and secondly to come constantly to Jesus for forgiveness (sanctified), that is to 'wash their feet'. He also went on to encourage them to wash one another's feet, that is to forgive each other constantly, just as he forgave them.

Now we need to return to the passage from 1 John: 'If we claim to be without sin, we deceive ourselves and the truth is not in us. If we confess our sins, he is faithful and just and will forgive us our sins and purify us from all unrighteousness' (1 Jn 1:8–9). Can we now understand better what John is referring to? No Christian retains an inherently sinful nature. He is justified before God, who sees him as holy. However, each time he sins he becomes impure, and needs to have his feet washed again. Christians who have learned the secret of a humble life are doing this constantly. An evil thought may be harboured for a minute or two, but then it is at once repented of, and 'Sorry, Lord. Forgive me' washes the feet again. Fellowship with God is instantly restored. An unkind remark can be left to fester, but the humble Christian immediately

asks the offended party for their forgiveness, and there is
harmony again.

When John is referring to those who continue to sin, he
means those who have forgotten that they need to come
constantly back to God. These continue to sin without
being repentant of it. They continue *in* their sins. And
ultimately, of course, that will lead to death:

> If anyone sees his brother commit a sin that does not lead to
> death, he should pray and God will give him life. I refer to
> those whose sin does not lead to death. There is a sin that
> leads to death. I am not saying that he should pray about that.
> All wrongdoing is sin, and there is sin that does not lead to
> death (1 Jn 5:16–17).

So there are two types of sin—that which leads to death,
which is the 'needing-a-bath' type, where the person is
unsaved. And there is the sin which doesn't lead to
death—the 'needing-to-wash-feet' type. The prayer that
he is referring to is the forgiveness that we can bring to
each other—Jesus said that we should wash one another's
feet. But we cannot save one another. Only God can do
that. Of course we can and should pray that unbelievers be
saved, but we cannot make it happen.

Again, in Hebrews we read: 'If we deliberately keep on
sinning after we have received the knowledge of the truth,
no sacrifice for sins is left, but only a fearful expectation
of judgment and of raging fire that will consume the
enemies of God' (Heb 10:26–27). To keep on sinning
deliberately means that we no longer return to God for
forgiveness, that the sin remains with us, that we are
unrepentant of those sins that we continue to commit,
and therefore there is no sacrifice left, because Jesus did
not die for the unrepentant.

More prosaically, perhaps it can all be summarised like
this: Dirty feet don't stop me from being my Father's son,

but they do prevent me from walking into his living room!
Of course, if I let them stink long enough, I may get
kicked out of the house!

Internal purification

Now let us return from our excursion, and turn again to the
purifying fire of God, and see how to apply what we have
just learned.

We know that Holy Fire destroys the unholy and edifies
the holy. Until now, we would have said that if I had come
in a sinful state to my Father in heaven, I would have been
totally destroyed by the power of that fire. Now we need to
qualify that statement. First, of course, Jesus died for us
even when we were dead in our sins, which means that an
unbeliever can come to the Father in repentance, by faith
in the blood of Jesus, and he is not destroyed—otherwise
everyone would be destroyed. That much is already
obvious.

Secondly, as we have now seen, a believer, already
justified but with a contamination of today's sins upon
him, can come to the Father in the same way, repentant
and trusting in the blood of Jesus to 'wash his feet'. This
then is how the purifying fire is at work in those who
believe.

Because the fire destroys the unholy, it can do so within
the life of the believer, whose life is preserved through the
death of Jesus, but whose continuing sinfulness requires
the perfecting work of the Holy Spirit. Thus the Holy Fire
is a purifying fire.

*There cannot be a work of purification in an unbeliever,
because it would be like trying to separate black from
black.* As we saw from the basic principles of cleansing,
there must be differentiation for cleansing to take place.
So first he must be saved, then the process of purification

can begin. It is a natural consequence of the indwelling of
the Holy Fire.

So then although the Holy Fire is present, his work is far
from completed. We discovered the same thing when we
were discussing the situation of demons in the previous
chapter. A believer is only sanctified as far and as fast as
he will allow the Holy Spirit to work in his soul life, ie, his
flesh life. The yolk of the egg must grow and the white
must be eaten up. 'He must become greater; I must
become less,' said John the Baptist (Jn 3:30).

As this process continues, changes take place in the life
of the believer: 'To the pure, all things are pure, but to
those who are corrupted and do not believe, nothing is
pure. In fact, both their minds and consciences are corrupted' (Tit 1:15).

As we become purer, through the action of the fire of
God in our lives, so our minds and consciences are
improved. We are not only able to understand with the
mind of Christ, but to test all things through our consciences, knowing by the Spirit within us whether they
are righteous and true. Once we have a purified conscience, we have the mind of Christ and can distinguish
right from wrong. The Holy Spirit does this purifying so
that we can live according to our conscience.

This is the work of the purifying fire. We see the
consequences—repentance, forgiveness, brokenness, perfection. But how does God apply the heat?

8

Trial by Fire

Jesus is the Baptiser: 'I baptise you with water for repentance. But after me will come one who is more powerful
than I, whose sandals I am not fit to carry. He will baptise
you with the Holy Spirit and with fire' (Mt 3:11). We have
seen that the fire of God *is* the Holy Spirit, but this passage
seems to speak of both the Holy Spirit *and* fire. Many
believe that the fire that John the Baptist was referring to
in the above passage is the fire of trial—the purifying fire
through which we must pass if we are to 'become blame-
less and pure, children of God without fault in a crooked
and depraved generation, in which you shine like stars in
the universe . . .' (Phil 2:15).

A fire is not a comfortable place to be. If we are to be
made pure by the Refiner's fire, we can expect trouble.
Jesus promised as much when he said, 'In this world you
will have trouble' (Jn 16:33). This world is not heaven. It
is a place where we are moulded, pummelled, decornered,
abraded, honed and polished. A painful business.

Do not believe the Christian who tells you, 'Be saved
and all your troubles will be over.' Nonsense! Your
troubles are just beginning. But now we do not have to
tackle them alone. Jesus followed the sentence, 'In this
world you will have trouble,' with, 'But take heart! I have
overcome the world.' Trouble, yes, but through it the
promise of victory. With Jesus, the trouble will not win.

105

This is how the refining fire works to perfect us. He uses three main methods.

Suffering

Much nonsense is promulgated today about suffering. Easy-chair Christianity is fed to an easy-chair generation. It is suggested that our God never brings trial or difficulty or pain or suffering, that all these things come from the devil, and that if only we had enough faith, or if we got busy casting them out hard enough they would go away! Such teaching is not only false but brings believers who are struggling with many trials under powerful condemnation and depression.

Let us be quite clear. The 'God of all comforts' is not a God of 'all comfortable'! God did not originally intend that we should suffer, but suffering is a natural consequence of the Fall. When sin entered the world, suffering entered the world, and like the innocent victim of a road accident, it is often the seemingly innocent who get hurt the most. (Though in fact of course none of us is innocent, as we all know.)

The God of the Bible I read does use suffering as the purifying fire. I do not believe that he merely takes his hands off his children so that the devil can have a go, as many argue from the first chapters of Job. God never takes his hands off his children. He has promised not to, because he loves us too much for that. But he does cause us to suffer on occasion, also because he loves us. This is made totally plain in Psalm 69:26, where David is complaining to God about those who are persecuting him and gloating over his suffering: 'For they persecute those you wound and talk about the pain of those you hurt' (Ps 69:26).

The 'you' in this scripture is God. David understood that God can and does cause suffering; that it is for a purpose—to refine and purify character, which is of far greater concern to God than flesh—and that the sin was not in the suffering, but in the gloating. It is not even sinful to cause someone to suffer. It depends upon the motivation.

Like many, I used to be a total coward about injections. When the doctor who was a family friend came to visit I would go into hiding! I remember to my shame one day, when I needed to have an injection, throwing a screaming fit for at least an hour before they finally wrestled me to the floor. That hour of fear was far worse than the final small jab, but the memory lives for ever! Although I am sure that my parents justly felt that my behaviour was disgraceful, I am also sure that they hurt because of what needed to be done, and hated to see me suffer. But that didn't mean they sent the doctor away with the injection not done. They persisted, and I thank God that they did.

Now many people seem to think that it is almost as though there are two Gods—a God of love and a God of justice. My nephew once asked me why it is that the God of the Old Testament seems to be so full of violence and terror, while the God of the New Testament is so full of love and gentleness! But the God of the Old and New Testaments hasn't changed. The use of suffering isn't confined to the 'Old Testament God', as though he is some alien monster who has repented! 'It is better, if it is God's will, to suffer for doing good than for doing evil' (1 Pet 3:17). Once again, it is absolutely without question that Peter is referring to occasions when the suffering *is* according to God's will.

The compassion and justice of God are shown working together in perfect harmony in this beautiful passage from Isaiah 30, which I quote at length because he says it far better than I ever could:

Yet the Lord longs to be gracious to you; he rises to show you compassion. For the Lord is a God of justice. Blessed are all who wait for him!

O people of Zion, who live in Jerusalem, you will weep no more. How gracious he will be when you cry for help! As soon as he hears, he will answer you. Although the Lord gives you the bread of adversity and the water of affliction, your teachers will be hidden no more; with your own eyes you will see them. Whether you turn to the right or to the left, your ears will hear a voice behind you, saying, 'This is the way; walk in it.' Then you will defile your idols overlaid with silver and your images covered with gold; you will throw them away like a menstrual cloth and say to them, 'Away with you!'

He will also send you rain for the seed you sow in the ground, and the food that comes from the land will be rich and plentiful. In that day your cattle will graze in broad meadows. The oxen and donkeys that work the soil will eat fodder and mash, spread out with fork and shovel. In the day of great slaughter, when the towers fall, streams of water will flow on every high mountain and every lofty hill. The moon will shine like the sun, and the sunlight will be seven times brighter, like the light of seven full days, when the Lord binds up the bruises of his people and heals the wounds he inflicted (Is 30:18–26).

Notice that it is the Lord who gives the bread of adversity; it is the Lord who inflicts the wounds which he himself then heals.

So how should we respond? Do we therefore not pray for the sick or suffering in case we are praying against God's will? By no means! Of course we pray for the sick and suffering. First, not all suffering is according to God's will, as the 'if' in 1 Peter 3:17 shows. The 'if' implies clearly that there is an 'if not'. In which case, let us pray and see the work of Satan destroyed. Much suffering *is* a direct consequence of other problems. There are many cases on record of people who have been suffering from a disease such as arthritis. When it has been pointed out to them (through a word of knowledge, for example) that they need to forgive someone and they have done so, the disease disappears.

I remember listening to the testimony of a lady at a crusade we held in Brazil. Her thirty-year-old daughter had been totally blind since the age of one. She herself had been involved in witchcraft all that time. During the meeting, she repented and gave her life to the Lord. When we later prayed a general prayer for the sick, the woman's witchcraft necklace spontaneously broke and fell to the ground. In the same moment her daughter instantly received her sight, and was completely healed, just as Jesus himself set free the crippled lady in Luke 13 whom Satan had kept bound for eighteen long years.

Many people say that if Satan causes suffering *and* God causes suffering it doesn't seem fair, and how are we to know who has caused the suffering anyway? Remember the blind man about whom the disciples asked, 'Who is it that sinned, this man or his parents, that he should have been born blind?' What was the Lord's reply? '"Neither this man nor his parents sinned," said Jesus, "but this happened so that the work of God might be displayed in his life"' (Jn 9:3).

I do not believe that it is our place to be too philosophical when confronted with the sick and suffering. No one is helped if we go into a theological funk every time we are faced with a need. Jesus commanded his disciples: 'Heal the sick.' Let us pray for them and expect God to heal them. He does answer prayers! If we do not see an immediate healing, then we keep praying. But there are occasions when God uses suffering, and we can suffer according to God's will, just as the man born blind had to suffer with that crippling infirmity all his early life 'so that the work of God might be displayed in his life'. That too seems unfair if we are to judge God's actions from a merely medical viewpoint. But God is not an unfair God, and he has a far wider viewpoint than just our physical wellbeing, even though he cares about that too.

Suffering can cause us to become depressed, bitter and resentful. But if we allow the Holy Fire to do his work, we will overcome these things and become instead gentle, patient, kind, joyful in affliction and even thankful *for* our difficulties, not just *in spite* of them. For suffering adds a dimension to character which brings a far greater testimony. *Grace through trial touches the heartstrings of the world*. It is the stuff heroes are made of.

As we have said, God is far more concerned with perfecting the character of a person—breaking down the 'flesh' so that the spirit shines through—refining with his purifying fire the person who will live for eternity in heaven. Surely any amount of trouble or suffering is worth that.

Sacrifice

The other day I came across this proverb: 'Measure your success by what you had to give up to get it.'

Sacrifice must cost, or it is not sacrifice. David refused to accept the offer of the threshing floor from Araunah in 1 Chronicles 21, since he would not sacrifice an offering that had cost him nothing. We have studied the purpose of sacrifice in Chapter 3, so here we are only concerned to see how sacrifice is used by the purifying fire to perfect the believer.

While suffering is the involuntary 'crucifixion of the flesh', sacrifice is the voluntary laying down of otherwise desirable things. Fasting, avoiding the unspiritual, giving, mercy, worship and praise to God, doing good and sharing with others are all biblical examples of sacrifice which edify the giver, or rather the giver-up. The Spirit is trying to shine through the murk of our soul. The light is trying to penetrate the opacity. There is a confrontation of interests: 'For the sinful nature desires what is contrary to the Spirit, and the Spirit what is contrary to the sinful nature. They are in conflict with each other, so that you do not do what you want' (Gal 5:17).

The sinful nature will always pull us down, but we must fight it, although it is not comfortable to do so. The fire is at work. (Of course we cannot extrapolate this into saying that if it is uncomfortable it therefore must be good. That is Stoicism, not sacrifice.)

Paul exhorts us to purify ourselves from everything that contaminates body and spirit. This is a deliberate act, brought about by a decision to make the personal sacrifices necessary to perfect holiness, out of reverence for God. For each of us this sacrifice takes a different form. For example, my wife and I choose not to have a television in the house. This is not because we disapprove of it. Quite the opposite. But we know ourselves well enough to know that we would both spend too many hours distracted by it, and hence fewer hours in fellowship with God. (You may have guessed that we don't have children—then it would be sacrifice indeed!) Others fast one day a week, which we do not do. Some pray through the night regularly, sacrificing sleep. We are certainly not into that level of sacrifice! Still others give many precious hours visiting the sick and the elderly.

Each of us should be prepared to follow the guiding of the Holy Spirit and make the sacrifices he is calling us to; not becoming condemned because others seem to be better at it than us, but simply obeying his prompting. Struggle though it is, we become the purer for it.

Obedience

> Now that you have purified yourselves by obeying the truth so
> that you have sincere love for your brothers, love one another
> deeply, from the heart (1 Pet 1:22).

In early 1993, my wife and I had been sent to prepare a
crusade in Surabaya, in the country of Indonesia. It is a
thriving city in a steamy, tropical climate, and we needed
to live there for about six months. Soon after we arrived,
therefore, we began to hunt for a house to rent. Short-term
rentals were scarce, but within a few days we found a
small but simple house on the edge of town in a rather
plain neighbourhood. It was typically Indonesian: no hot
water, a tiled water tank in the bathroom from which one
dipped water for ablutions, and an outside kitchen. Not
elegant living, but adequate. At least the bedrooms had
air-conditioning! We liked the quiet situation, and felt
comfortable about it, so we accepted the proffered accom-
modation and promised to sign the contract the following
day.

That evening some Christian friends appeared, crying,
'Come with us!' and off we went into the sultry night
without further explanation. We passed through the beautiful end of town, and stopped outside a huge mansion. A
security guard saluted our arrival as we went inside. Here
were marble floors, chandeliers, spacious living rooms, a
fully-fitted 'Western-style' kitchen and gleaming bath-
rooms, hot water and air-conditioning throughout. 'It's
yours,' they said, 'free of charge for as long as you
want. It belongs to a Christian friend who is living in
Jakarta, and he wants to bless you.' We were speechless,
mumbling our amazed gratitude.

Back in our room, I couldn't sleep. I tossed and turned.
Something was wrong. I felt unhappy about the mansion,
though I couldn't see how we could refuse such an

amazing gift. Besides, everything about it was perfect, and exactly what we had prayed for. Still I felt troubled. In the morning I shared this concern with my wife Bron, and we prayed about it. God spoke to us clearly, and we realised that to take this house would mean breaking our word to the owner of the small house. It was a big temptation that we must refuse. 'But how can we explain to our generous Christian brothers that we are turning down such an offer?' we asked. The reply came, 'Be truthful.' So in trepidation we went back to them and explained, saying that the Holy Spirit had convicted us that we must remain true to our word and accept the contract on the first house, even though the second was by far the better. We must obey the Holy Spirit.

I thank God we did. We returned to sign the contract and pay our rent. During the interview we discovered that the owner of the small house was a widow. The rent on this house was her only income. It had been empty for six months and she was desperate. That same night she had had a second offer, which she had turned down because she had given her word to us.

> Beware of the teachers of the law. They like to walk around in flowing robes and love to be greeted in the market-places and have the most important seats in the synagogues and the places of honour at banquets. They devour widows' houses and for a show make lengthy prayers. Such men will be punished most severely (Lk 20:46–47).

Truly God had saved us from a dreadful mistake by convincing us of the need to be obedient to the truth. Through this we grew in spirit, even though for the next six months we had to make the sacrifice of less elegant living. As it happened, we had some wonderful and amusing times in that little house, which I wouldn't have given up for anything. We were content there, as I

believe we always are if we learn to accept God's will for
our lives.

*Simple obedience is never simple. But true obedience is
the secret of a tender heart.* Samuel tells us: 'To obey is
better than sacrifice' (1 Sam 15:22).

Obedience, of course, means obedience to the truth, as
we read above in 1 Peter 1:22, 'Now that you have
purified yourselves by obeying the truth . . .' Instead of
obedience to the strict Mosaic law, which never truly
cleansed but only covered up, we are now obedient to
the Word of God himself, which is Jesus Christ. This is
a purifying process: 'For the word of God is living and
active. Sharper than any double-edged sword, it penetrates
even to dividing soul and spirit, joints and marrow; it
judges the thoughts and attitudes of the heart (Heb 4:12).

The Word penetrates, divides and judges. In other
words, there is differentiation, separation and removal
(by judgement)—all the features of the purification process. But to allow this to happen requires submission to
him. Thankfully this is not merely a passive resignation,
because the Word is living and active, powerful to coun-
ter-attack the active force of destruction, and powerful for
the restoration of the divine order through the work of the
purifying fire.

In summary, then, purification is a process of restoration. God forgives through the blood of Christ, through the
action of justification and through purification. The purifying fire works in the life of the believer to perfect him,
by breaking down the sinful nature to allow the Spirit, the
Holy Fire, to shine through. The normal methods God uses
are suffering, sacrifice and obedience. All are manifestations of the purifying fire. All will lead us into a greater
love and understanding of the wonderful glory awaiting
us, if we remain faithful.

Having established these glorious truths—the restoration of our full fellowship with the Holy Spirit, and his consequent work of purification of our souls—which are at the heart of God's redemptive plan for mankind, we can now return to Matthew 3: 'He will baptise you with the Holy Spirit and with fire' (v. 11). John meant far more than purification when he spoke of the baptism by fire. That is only half the story, and we need to look at the other half, because it will lead us into astonishing discoveries and a new chapter.

9

Eternal Fire (Part 1)

Hell and Judgement

We arose before dawn. It was damp and cold, but sounds of movement penetrated the hut from the darkness outside. A horse snorted, and muffled voices hung in the silence. We dressed quickly, and joined other yawning shadows. The moist air was heavy with the fetid scent of manure. Before long we were seated on our small mountain horses, creaking uncomfortably on slippery saddles. The torches of the Indonesian guides stretched out ahead, revealing the course of the twisting mountain path. We began lurchingly downhill, unable to anticipate the sudden dips and jerks of our sure-footed mounts in the blackness.

The eastern sky held the promise of the coming day, grey above the inky black horizon of the mountain still hiding our progress. We levelled onto a broad plain, and the going was easier. Weird shapes of scattered cacti and small shrubs slid by. The horse in front was now more than just a scuffle of footsteps—a shadow blending into the gloom. Apart from the sounds of our journey, the world was totally still. We entered a thin mist, which emphasised the eerie deserted surroundings. The mountain had a feeling of foreboding, and I shivered again, wondering why we had chosen to come.

There were about twenty of us, tourists, lured by curiosity to view Mount Bromo—which means Fire Mountain—one of the active volcanoes in the backbone of Java. We should be there at dawn, we were told, and on we rode, damp with dew, each one shrouded in the cloud of his own private counsel. The caravan was climbing, now over sand, now over lava heaps, huge bubbles of rock long since solid and cold. Here all was barren, void of life.

The mountainside ahead loomed high above us. People were dismounting, snatches of conversation bringing dawn to our souls. From here we walked. Up again into the lightening sky, soon breathlessly counting step after ponderous step. Now, as sharp premonition, we caught a draft of the acrid stink of sulphur. We emerged at last onto the high lip of the crater, and looked down into the throat of hell.

Hell is not a popular subject. It has been misrepresented by preachers, misunderstood by generations, discarded as anachronistic thinking by modernists, 'demythologised' by theologians, lampooned by the media, feared and avoided as a subject by almost everyone. No one enjoys discussing even such necessary but temporary unpleasantness as a visit to the dentist, so it is hardly surprising that the majority of Christians are poorly taught on the subject. How many of us have bought or even read a book on hell? When was the last sermon you heard on it? And was it a genuine attempt to look at what the Bible teaches, or simply an apology for a bit of doctrine that God shouldn't have invented?

The journey described above left an indelible memory in my mind. The smoke-black, cracked crater wall seemed almost sheer down to the glow of the furnace below. A strange orange light echoed off the tortured rocks on the edge of the pit. Fumes spiralled upwards and the smell of sulphur was overpowering. The knowledge that the mountain was, and horrifyingly still is, being used for child sacrifice was not the only reason for its general sense of evil. It was an awful place, and we left it with no regrets. Under the soft dawn sky, the gentle gleaming sun provided a stunning contrast to the raw fierceness of the crater. And yet God made it. . . .

I have a recurring picture of the world chattering and laughing up that mountain as carefree as tourists, cameras a-jangle, and falling headlong over the sheer cliff-face into the raging fire below. For ever. I see myself running down the throng, desperate with warning, and, like the leaden feet that will not run from the fire in our dreams, helpless with impotence to stop the relentless crowd. Oh, please God, somehow we must stop them.

For that is what hell means. Such judgement does not sit comfortably with our image of gentle Jesus, meek and mild. For centuries man has wrestled with this contradiction, and has invented diverse and ingenious means of drawing the teeth of hell, turning it into a waiting-room, or a blank nothingness, or removing it altogether. But none of these accords with the teaching of the Bible, and specifically of our Lord Jesus himself.

I rejoice that our studies so far can be extended and applied to this much-maligned subject, bringing a clearer light, so that the rubbish of distorted thinking can be discarded and we can view God's purpose from a fuller perspective. Let us see what we can discover.

Despite my earlier questions, good books have been written on hell, so I now want to take no more than a quick, general overview of hell and some of the false teachings, so that we can use our understanding of the Holy Fire of God to clarify some of these mistakes. Then in the next chapter we will study the lake of fire, to try to discover exactly what it is.

God of love, God of judgement

I think at some time all of us have asked the question: If God is love (which he is), how then can he allow people to suffer in hell for ever? This doesn't seem just or fair. Surely God must ultimately allow everyone to be saved? Or at the very least, not perpetuate hell for ever? If God is a God of forgiveness, surely he must ultimately forgive everyone? This line of thinking has led to several 'isms' which we should know a little about.

What hell is not

The first error is *Universalism*. Many scholars have been adherents of this doctrine, and it is still very popular today, especially among liberal theologians, who do not feel constrained to accept Scripture at its face value. Basically it says that Jesus is the Saviour of the world, therefore all men are or will eventually be saved, otherwise the work of Jesus could not be finished, as he declared it to be on the cross.

If we stuck to just a few scriptures out of context, this is a very appealing thought, and would mean we can all rest more securely in our future.

However, the great body of teaching in the Bible contradicts it. I don't want to get deeply into a theology refuting this thinking, merely to register that this thinking exists. One scripture will suffice. In Matthew 25, Jesus tells a very graphic parable about the sheep and the goats, which is hardly a parable at all, so close is it to reality. He castigates the unrighteous for their failure to love, concluding: 'Then they will go away to eternal punishment, but the righteous to eternal life' (Mt 25:46).

It is very hard to wriggle out of such clarity without diminishing the teaching or the character of Christ. No, we must face the fact that God is a God of judgement, and that some will go to hell, and they will be there for ever. Without this understanding, of course, our incentive for evangelism wanes into platitudes.

The second great 'ism' is *annihilationism*. This is probably the most commonly held view about hell today in the West, both across non-Christian and Christian (yes and even evangelical) worlds. The idea is that separation from God must be the greatest hell that anyone can imagine, and that therefore after the judgement (which, it is argued, is the fire) those condemned will evaporate into the void of separation. They simply cease to exist. Anything more than this, we are told, would be both vindictive of God and a failure of the loving-kindness of God, who couldn't possibly allow anyone to endure eternal punishment. This is an understandable view coming out of a 'feel-good' generation which prefers to think on the bright side of things, but it is not supported by what we read in the Bible.

Again, one scripture will suffice to refute this. Notice that I draw this also from the teaching of Jesus himself, and from the bits which are accepted even by liberals as being the 'most authentic' sections we have: 'And if your eye causes you to sin, pluck it out. It is better for you to enter the kingdom of God with one eye than to have two eyes and be thrown into hell, where "their worm does not die, and the fire is not quenched"' (Mk 9:47–48).

Jesus, quoting Isaiah 66, describes hell in graphic and alarming detail, and no space is left for those who don't like the idea of punishment, or of it being eternal. These words cannot be misinterpreted, unless one comes to the Scripture with a personal preconception, determined to make it fit with one's own ideas. Then, of course, anything can be explained away, as it so often is. No, if we read it like it is and *then* interpret it, we are left with one inescapable conclusion. The Bible, and Jesus, teach that there is an eternal fire of punishment into which the unrighteous will be thrown after the judgement, and in which they will remain for eternity.

The third great deception is simply that hell doesn't exist at all; that there is no 'void of separation' and therefore no universal salvation. Allied with the Eastern and New Age idea that there is no such thing as evil, there is then no need for either hell or salvation from it. Now we have slipped completely off the rungs of anything which could be called Christian doctrine, and are falling into *pluralism*, or the tolerance of all religions. Just as the Assyrians, who 'spoke about the God of Jerusalem as they did about the gods of the other peoples of the world—the work of men's hands' (2 Chron 32:19) ridiculed Hezekiah for his faithfulness to the Lord, so the multi-cultural, multi-racial society of today looks with severe disapproval upon those who remain dogmatic about their own faith. Labelled 'exclusivism' and described as the 'I-am-right-and-everyone-else-is-wrong' syndrome, it is painted as the severest form of bigotry, and not to be tolerated. Hezekiah-style unswerving faithfulness is called 'narrow-minded dogmatism'.

This intolerance is extended both to Christians who take their faith literally and seriously (labelled 'fundamentalists') and incidentally to Jews who do too. This results in consequent ridicule and persecution of born-again Bible-believing Christians and fundamental Judaism. It rapidly degenerates into the very hypocrisy of which it is supposed to be so critical. And, of course, anti-Judaism is anti-Semitism. The author of this thinking then begins to show his true colours. *Pluralism is a satanic plot to deny the truth of Scripture and the uniqueness of Jesus Christ.* But again the Bible is unequivocal: 'Jesus answered, "I am the way and the truth and the life. No-one comes to the Father except through me" ' (Jn 14:6).

If hell doesn't exist, that then begs another question. What *does* happen after death? If there is no hell and no 'nothingness', either we all end up in heaven (Universalism), or something else happens. About the only option remaining is to go round in circles. So half the world today believes in reincarnation. Not only is it the basis of the Hindu religion, but it is becoming increasingly popular in the West, especially among those who espouse the New Age movement. Again I do not wish to describe this error in detail, except to say that it is once again contrary to the whole of the Bible. Hebrews 9:27 is well known: 'Just as man is destined to die once, and after that to face judgment . . . .' We die once, and therefore cannot go round again to die a second time. And if this alternative is so clearly refuted in the Bible, we come back to its original teaching. Eternal heaven and eternal hell.

No doting grandfather

In fact, a God of love *must* also be a God who judges unrighteousness. Pure love must abhor sin. As we have seen from the previous chapter, it is not enough simply to be separated from sin, but the sin must be destroyed if purification is to occur, and love to remain pure. Therefore a God of love has to be also a God of justice and judgement. He has to make provision for the destruction of the impure if he is to remain pure. Impurity would tarnish not only his love, but also his glory.

In his excellent book *Crucial Questions about Hell*, Ajith Fernando explains that for God not to judge unrighteousness would be to diminish his glory, and that anything which does so is to the detriment of all creation. Sin is an affront to his glory. He goes on to say: 'Judgment enhances his glory by responding adequately to affronts to this glory. Because acting to enhance his glory is essentially a benevolent act which seeks the best for creation, judgment too is a benevolent act.'[1]

Of course, the power and glory of God are such that it is

totally impossible that anything could stain his character. Any stain is instantly destroyed. He is by nature a self-purifying God. Therefore judgement and hell are an inevitable consequence of his character, not merely an uncomfortable add-on extra. They are just as much a part of God's creation as heaven is. They have to be.

We have already seen that the Holy Fire of God instantly destroys all that is unholy. Immediately then we remove one of the great imponderables, which is how God can choose to allow some to burn eternally in hell. God's character is such that no other course is possible. Sin is destroyed as soon as it comes into the presence of the Holy Fire of the living God. That destruction is a foregone conclusion. Judgement can therefore be seen in this light. It is the inevitable, automatic outworking of the Holy Fire. It is not some inexplicable and rather unpleasant thing that God has unwillingly decided to do to the unrighteous. It is the power of God in action—the power that we have already seen and described—and the inevitable consequence of dying in one's sins. *How dare we think that we can come into his holy presence in a sinful state and escape destruction?*

These few paragraphs have led us to see that however much we may wriggle, we must face the truth. We see in fact that our very desire to squirm at these thoughts is wrong, and that we can and should give God the glory for his righteous judgements, because by them he is demonstrating his holiness. He is not some doting grandfather who is unable or unwilling to discipline his grandchildren. Nor is he some benign and feeble judge, whose every verdict is, 'Never mind!' and whose every sentence is, 'Off you go.' He is the Holy and Righteous One, the Awesome and Jealous God, the Consuming Fire, to whom every knee will bow, and from whose judgement none will escape. 'After this I heard what sounded like the roar of a great multitude in heaven shouting: "Hallelujah! Salvation and glory and power belong to our God, for true and just are his judgments" ' (Rev 19:1–2a).

What is hell like?

Having established that hell exists, we can ask: What is it like? What seems a simple question becomes as involved as a detective story.

Hell is described in many different ways: raging fire, burning sulphur, outer darkness, gloomy dungeons, a gigantic furnace, the place of the dead, destruction, the land of oblivion, cut off from God, separated from God, in the presence of God! It all seems so contradictory. When the Bible appears to contradict itself, it is time to dig deeper! To come down on one or other side of the argument is to miss the truth which lies hidden beneath, and which enables both to be true. That is the truth we are searching for.

Let us begin with a brief word study. In the King James Version 'hell' is derived from the Hebrew word *Sheol*. The New International Version usually renders this word as 'the grave', and doesn't use the word 'hell' in the Old Testament at all. *Sheol* meant 'the unseen state, the place of the dead, a dark, gloomy place where the dead lie silent', 'no more remembered by God' (Ps 88:5, KJV). Later in the same psalm we read: 'Is your love declared in the grave, your faithfulness in Destruction? Are your wonders known in the place of darkness, or your righteous deeds in the land of oblivion?' (Ps 88:11–12).

Again we meet an inconsistency—destruction (Hebrew, *Abaddon*) hardly matches with darkness or 'the land of oblivion'. There seems to be two states of hell: darkness and oblivion on the one hand, and destruction on the other. It doesn't make sense.

When we turn to the New Testament, it gets even more complicated! Referring in Matthew 25 to the judgement to come, Jesus speaks of both outer darkness ('And throw that worthless servant outside, into the darkness, where there will be weeping and gnashing of teeth'—v. 30) and eternal fire ('Then he will say to those on his left, "Depart from me, you who are cursed, into the eternal fire prepared for the devil and his angels"'—v. 41). How do we reconcile these? First of all we need to define our terms. As we do so, we open a real Pandora's box.

In the Greek there are three words which we translate as 'hell' in the NIV. These are *Hades*, *Gehenna* and *Tartarus*. We also need to note the word *Abussos*, which means 'the Abyss', or 'bottomless pit'. Could these all be the same place, ie, are they all different words for the same thing? Or are they all different places? Are they in fact referring to a physical place? Or perhaps they are a spiritual state? Or both? Let us look at them in reverse order.

The Abyss and Tartarus

The Greek word *Tartarus* only occurs once in Scripture, in 2 Peter 2:4, and it is clearly a place of remand: 'God did not spare angels when they sinned, but sent them to hell [*Tartarus*], putting them into gloomy dungeons to be held for judgment.' These sinning angels are the demons, who presumably are no longer free to roam the earth but await their final judgement in confinement.

We find something similar with the Abyss (*Abussos*). In the story of the Gadarene madman, the demons knew about it and feared it: 'And they begged him repeatedly not to order them to go into the Abyss' (Lk 8:31). It means 'a bottomless pit' and is described further in Revelation as a place of fire: 'When [the angel] opened the Abyss, smoke rose from it like the smoke from a gigantic furnace. The sun and sky were darkened by the smoke from the Abyss' (Rev 9:2). It is the place where Satan will be locked, as it were, under house arrest for the thousand years (Rev 20:3). The beast will come up out of it and go to his destruction (Rev 17:8). In both instances it seems that the Abyss is also a temporary holding place like *Tartarus*, and there is no reason to believe that they are not the same place, except that one is described as 'gloomy dungeons' and the other 'a gigantic furnace'. If they are different, it seems clear that both will be redundant after the judgement, when they have served their purpose. We will see.

Gehenna

Gehenna is a Greek version of the original Hebrew *Ge Hinnom* which means 'Valley of Hinnom'. More commonly referred to as Ben Hinnom, it was the valley to the south of Jerusalem where Topheth was located, which had originally been the place of sacrifice to the god Molech, where children were thrown into the fire: 'They have built the high places of Topheth in the Valley of Ben Hinnom to burn their sons and daughters in the fire—something I did not command, nor did it enter my mind' (Jer 7:31).

It was desecrated by Josiah, reinstated, then later apparently became the general rubbish dump of the city, in which fires burned continuously, rather like Smoky Mountain outside Manila. In Jesus' day it represented a place of destruction, with evil overtones. Jesus used it regularly as a graphic description of the eternal fire and final place of destruction. Interestingly the word is only used on one other occasion, when James is speaking specifically of fire in James 3:6. This Gehenna, then, is a place of fire, and represents the fiercest judgement of God.

Jesus speaks of Gehenna eleven times[2] and he is always

referring to destruction or judgement, with the possible exception of Matthew 23:15, when he calls the hypocrites 'sons of hell'. But we will see shortly that this too is confirmation of the concept of Gehenna being a place of fire.

In Matthew 5 and Mark 9, Jesus is teaching his disciples that it is better to enter life maimed than to go into hell (Gehenna), where the fire never goes out. Matthew 18 repeats the passage, referring to 'eternal fire' and Gehenna in parallel verses. He obviously means us to understand that Gehenna is an eternal fire.

Hades

'Hades' is used throughout the Septuagint (the Greek translation of the Old Testament) to translate the Hebrew word *Sheol*, and carries a similar meaning, that is, 'the place of the dead; the unseen state; the grave'. It is the place of the dead, but not of all the dead, for David praised God that he was delivered from Sheol: 'For great is your love towards me; you have delivered me from the depths of the grave' (Ps 86:13). He knew that he wouldn't end up in hell. Such is our assurance too as the redeemed of the Lord.

Jesus only refers to Hades on four occasions. On each occasion it could easily be translated as 'death' or as 'the grave', which concurs with what we have already found. Matthew 11:23 and Luke 10:15 are identical: 'And you, Capernaum, will you be lifted up to the skies? No, you will go down to the depths [Hades]' (Lk 10:15). In Matthew 16:18 he is telling Peter that the gates of Hades will not overcome the church. It will become clear later why Jesus used the word 'Hades' here and not 'Gehenna'.

Then we have the parable of the rich man and Lazarus in Luke 16. The rich man is described as being 'in hell [Hades], where he was in torment . . . ' (Lk 16:23), from where he cries out: "'Father Abraham, have pity on me and send Lazarus to dip the tip of his finger in water and cool my tongue, because I am in agony in this fire'" (Lk 16:24). So here we clearly see Hades also being described as a place of fire and torment.

Hades is also mentioned seven other times in the New Testament, either as a translation of Sheol when the Old Testament is being quoted, or, in the book of Revelation, in conjunction with death. Here Hades is almost personi- fied, but is never referred to as a place of final destruction. That seems to be the exclusive right of Gehenna.

And then in Revelation 20 we find something very interesting: 'The sea gave up the dead that were in it, and death and Hades gave up the dead that were in them, and each person was judged according to what he had done. Then death and Hades were thrown into the lake of fire. The lake of fire is the second death' (Rev 20:13– 14). This is the description of the final judgement. The final act of that judgement, before the coming of the new heaven and the new earth, is the destruction of death and Hades in the lake of fire. If the one, Hades, is destroyed in the other, then they are two different places, or two different spiritual states. They cannot be the same. Hades therefore is a temporary place.

I feel like the detective who has been following up a routine theft only to come across a nest of drug dealers. It wasn't the answer we were looking for, because we were asking the wrong question. But it has brought us to an amazing truth.

Now the pieces of the jigsaw begin to fall into place. As we have seen, Hades cannot be the same as the eternal fire. But Gehenna is clearly described by Jesus as just that. If the lake of fire is eternal, then Gehenna is the lake of fire, and it cannot be the same place or state as Hades, which as we have seen is thrown *into* the lake of fire. We will be looking at the lake of fire in more detail. For the moment, we realise that Hades and Gehenna are not the same.

So Hades is a temporary place where the unrighteous are held awaiting the final judgement, when they are given up. However, it also remains a place of torment. This exactly describes what we find in 2 Peter 2: 'If this is so, then the Lord knows how to rescue godly men from trials and to hold the unrighteous for the day of judgment, *while continuing their punishment*' (v. 9, my emphasis).

This is the same passage where we read that the angels who sinned were being held in judgement in hell, that is *Tartarus*. So it seems that *Tartarus*/Abyss and Hades are one and the same. Their descriptions and purposes exactly match. For convenience, therefore, from now on I will refer to them as simply Hades. It represents a temporary state of divine punishment, and that is where the unrighteous will go when they die. But they are not the place of final destruction; Satan is held there, then released. The demons are awaiting judgement. The beast will come up out of the Abyss and then go to his destruction.

Now that we have established that there are two states of existence which are both described as 'hell' in the Bible, we need to ask further questions. What is the purpose of having two states? Surely all those who die in their sins could be instantly destroyed in the lake of fire? Also, if those in Hades still have to be judged, but are already known to be guilty, what is the purpose of the final judgement? And what about those who have died in Christ? To find the answers, we need to understand what is actually happening at the final judgement.

The final judgement

Let us look at Revelation 20 in more detail as it explains what will happen when all the dead are finally judged:

> Then I saw a great white throne and him who was seated on it. Earth and sky fled from his presence, and there was no place for them. And I saw the dead, great and small, standing before the throne, and books were opened. Another book was opened, which is the book of life. The dead were judged according to what they had done as recorded in the books. The sea gave up the dead that were in it, and death and Hades gave up the dead that were in them, and each person was judged according to what he had done. Then death and Hades were thrown into the lake of fire. The lake of fire is the second death. If anyone's name was not found written in the book of life, he was thrown into the lake of fire (Rev 20:11–15).

Here are two groups of people coming from three places. They come from the sea, from death and from Hades. In Jewish tradition, and throughout the Scriptures, the sea is a 'type' or symbol of death, which explains its presence in this group. Everyone who has ever died is therefore brought before the throne.

Jesus tells us that he will come again, and that only then will everyone be judged together. Until that time comes, they must be held awaiting judgement somewhere! We have already seen that the guilty are held in Hades. What of those who are in Christ? Obviously they cannot also be held there, as the parable of Lazarus and the rich man makes clear. Jesus said that Lazarus was with Abraham: 'And besides all this, between us and you [the rich man] a great chasm has been fixed, so that those who want to go from here to you cannot, nor can anyone cross over from there to us' (Lk 16:26).

So those who die in Christ must be held somewhere else. That somewhere is heaven, but not the final heaven. Are we now saying that there are two heavens as well?[3] Revelation 21 says that after the judgement there will be a new heaven and a new earth, so it seems that those whose names are in the book of life will be held in the old heaven until the judgement. But what then is its purpose if people are already in heaven or Hades?

Let it be clear that the final judgement is not about whether the dead will go to heaven or hell. That is already determined by whether their names are in the book of life. That is not the point. The dead are being judged *according to what they have done* which is recorded in 'the books'. This judgement is not to decide whether they are guilty or not, but to decide the severity of the sentence, or their position of elevation in heaven.

For there will be places and a hierarchy in heaven, and indeed in hell also. When James and John asked Jesus if they may sit at his right hand when he came into his kingdom, he didn't explain that all would be equal, but said that those places were not his to grant, thereby implicitly confirming that they exist. Furthermore, the Lord's exhortation to 'lay up treasure in heaven' becomes meaningless unless there is a variation in level of reward there; that is, it must be worth something to us when we get there. It cannot mean buying our way into heaven with good works, because we go by grace not works. The only possibility remaining is that our treasure in heaven will be a reward once we are there, according to the amount we have laid up. Paul confirms this argument in 1 Corinthians 3: 'The fire will test the quality of each man's work. If what he has built survives, he will receive his reward. If it is burned up, he will suffer loss; he himself will be saved, but only as one escaping through the flames' (vv. 13–15).

If our work for the Lord, which is our treasure in heaven, is made of straw and burned up, we do not lose our salvation since we are saved by grace, but we are saved only by the skin of our teeth! We may end up being the doorkeeper, but we will not be sitting at the right or left hand of Jesus! (But just to be there will be wonderful beyond our imagining!)

Similarly, there are levels of sinfulness which it seems will receive different levels of punishment. In Matthew 11, Jesus explains that there will be different levels of suffering at the judgement: 'But I tell you that it will be more bearable for Sodom on the day of judgment than for you' (Mt 11:24).

The nearest parallel I can think of is that being in Hades is like a prisoner who has been to trial, been found guilty, but is then held in prison awaiting his final sentence by the judge. The verdict from the jury was 'guilty'. It is only the severity of his sentence which remains to be finalised. And if anyone's name is not found written in the book of life, he will be thrown into the lake of fire.

It also makes sense that if there are places in heaven and hell to be allocated, then the judgement cannot take place until all are judged together. By then death and Hades will have served their purpose and, being evil places, they will be thrown into the lake of fire as well. All will then be finished, and the way will be clear for the new heaven and new earth. But exactly what *is* this lake of fire if it is not hell?

Notes

1. Ajith Fernando, *Crucial Questions about Hell* (Kingsway, 1991), p. 102.
2. Matthew 5:22; 5:29; 5:30; 10:28; 18:9; 23:15; 23:33; Mark 9:43; 9:45; 9:47; Luke 12:5.
3. Actually we read about at least four. Paul was 'caught up to the third heaven', and that was before the final judgement when there will be a new one, which must be the fourth.

10

Eternal Fire (Part 2)

The Lake of Fire

Eternal destruction

We have already discovered that the punishment of the wicked is eternal. Paul describes it as 'everlasting destruction', which is in itself a physical impossibility, but evidently it is not a spiritual one! If then Hades is a temporary place and the final punishment of the unrighteous is eternal, then the lake of fire which is their final destiny must be eternal. That much is clear. Secondly, since both the lake of fire and Gehenna are described as places (or states) of eternal destruction, and nowhere is there any suggestion that there is more than one such place, they must be one and the same, as we have already surmised. We read in Revelation 18:8 that Babylon will be consumed by fire, and that 'the smoke from her goes up for ever' (Rev 19:3). *So, the lake of fire is the eternal fire.*

Burning sulphur has been a symbol of judgement since the time of Sodom and Gomorrah. Burning sulphur was prophesied in the Psalms, warned of by the prophets, and used to describe the lake of fire in the book of Revelation. Here it is variously called the 'fiery lake of burning sulphur', the 'lake of burning sulphur' and 'the lake of fire'. The wrath of God is regularly represented as fire, as we have seen, and here the lake of fire is the ultimate manifestation of the wrath of God; the final and eternal destruction of all that is evil. So where exactly does this lake of fire come from?

The breath of the Lord

There is no doubt that the wrath of God will destroy all that is evil, and will burn even down to hell: 'For a fire is kindled in mine anger, and shall burn unto the lowest hell, and shall consume the earth with her increase, and set on fire the foundations of the mountains' (Deut 32:22, KJV). But the reference here is to Sheol, which confirms that the fire of God burns there also. It doesn't tell us about the lake of fire, unless the term 'lowest hell', used by Moses, was the Hebrew equivalent of Gehenna before that valley was known.

We should look further. Let us turn to Isaiah 30. From verse 27 on, Isaiah is bringing a prophecy against the king of Assyria, the scourge of Israel, declaring that judgement and destruction await him. In verse 27 he speaks again of the tongue of the Lord being a 'consuming fire', an expression we are already well familiar with. He repeats this phrase in verse 30, and then goes on to describe the judgement being prepared for the king: 'Topheth has long been prepared; it has been made ready for the king. Its fire pit has been made deep and wide, with an abundance of fire and wood; the breath of the Lord, like a stream of burning sulphur, sets it ablaze' (Is 30:33).

Now Topheth is as we already know the place of sacrifice in the Valley of Ben Hinnom which Jesus called Gehenna, and which we have identified as being the lake of fire. Here we are told how that fire is set. It is the breath of the Lord, that is the Holy Fire, the consuming fire, which breathes upon the tinder in the fire pits of Gehenna, kindling the fire to receive the king of

Assyria. *The lake of fire is set alight by the breath of God*! The Holy Fire is the consuming fire which we read about throughout Scripture as the fire of destruction. There is, and can be, no other.

What *is* this lake of fire?

If this lake of burning sulphur is eternal, and it is set alight by the Holy Spirit, what actually is it? After the end of all things there will be no tinder to light, unless that tinder is the souls of the wicked, and Satan and his angels. But since they are all thrown *into* the lake of fire, the fire must already be prepared beforehand, and so must be something else.

Daniel 7 gives us the final, astonishing clue. In it the prophet describes a vision of four beasts, in which he saw the throne of God and God himself, the Ancient of Days, sitting upon it: 'His throne was flaming with fire, and its wheels were all ablaze. A river of fire was flowing, coming out from before him' (Dan 7:9–10).

Here Daniel describes the same river of fire that Isaiah speaks of—the stream of burning sulphur coming from the throne, the breath of God which we know to be the Holy Spirit. But now we see something else, for Daniel goes on: 'Then I continued to watch because of the boastful words the horn was speaking. I kept looking until the beast was slain and its body destroyed and thrown into the blazing fire' (Dan 7:11). In the context, this blazing fire is clearly the same river of fire that flowed from the throne of God. And the beast was thrown directly into it; not into something else that the river of fire had set alight.

Now let us compare this revelation in Daniel's vision with that of John who describes it like this: 'But the beast was captured, and with him the false prophet . . . The two of them were thrown alive into the fiery lake of burning sulphur' (Rev 19:20).

Daniel's vision of the final end of the beast was the same as John's. The beast was thrown into what is described as 'blazing fire' and 'the fiery lake of burning sulphur'. They must be one and the same. This fire is not simply *a* fire set alight by the Holy Spirit, but *the* fire coming from the throne of God. Before we come to the final and inevitable conclusion, let us review the properties of this lake of fire.

It is eternal. It is set by the breath of God. It flows from the throne of God. When the unrighteous enter it, they are instantly but eternally destroyed. These are all characteristics of the consuming fire that we have been studying throughout this book. We are left with one inescapable conclusion. Can we—dare we—infer that the lake of fire is the *same thing* as the consuming fire? That the lake of burning sulphur of the book of Revelation *is* the Holy Spirit?

Instantly too many objections come to mind.

The first is that it is inconceivable, blasphemous even, to suggest that the evil of hell should be associated with the holiness of God. They must be different places.

But as we have seen, God himself created both Hades and the lake of fire. Secondly, God himself lights the fire with the breath of his wrath. God himself is not afraid to confront and deal with evil, which he does by destroying it. That is all that is happening here. The only difference is that the destruction is an eternal destruction because the elements that need to be destroyed are eternal.

Separation from God

The second objection is that the Bible speaks about hell, the lake of fire, being eternal separation from God. If Satan and his demons, and all the unrighteous, the 'cowardly, the unbelieving, the vile, the murderers, the sexually immoral, those who practise magic arts, the idolaters and all liars'; if 'their place will be in the fiery lake of burning sulphur' (Rev 21:8); if they are being destroyed in the consuming fire, the Holy Spirit, then they are not separated, but in the presence of God. Surely that could not be?

We need to understand what separation means. We cannot say that God is in heaven, Satan is in hell, and that is the end of all things. That is simply not the teaching of the Bible. Satan is currently roaming throughout the earth; he is not in hell. He *will* be thrown into the Abyss for a thousand years, then released again, and finally thrown into the lake of fire. That is where he will remain for ever.

Neither is God confined to a 'place' called heaven. God is never confined. God *is*. He said, 'I am.' When all is finished, and the new heaven and new earth have come, God is. In Psalm 139 David graphically illustrates that there is nowhere we can go from the presence of God: 'If I ascend up into heaven, thou art there: if I make my bed in hell, behold, thou art there' (Ps 139:8, KJV).

Hell here is of course Sheol, but if God is present in Sheol, why not also in the lake of burning sulphur? We cannot run away from God and pretend that there are places where he isn't. He is everywhere, and that means in Hades and the lake of fire also.

Therefore separation from God is not a matter of where God is or where he isn't. As it has always meant since the fall of Adam, separation from God is a question of where *we* are. In the Garden of Eden, God was crying out to Adam, 'Where are you?' It is *we* who have become separated through sin. If that sin remains upon us in our death, and for ever, then our separation will be eternal in just the same way that although God and Adam were both in the garden, God had to cry out for Adam, because he

was apart from him, torn apart by sin. So what does being
separated from God mean?

Paul tells us in 2 Thessalonians:

> He will punish those who do not know God and do not obey
> the gospel of our Lord Jesus. They will be punished with
> everlasting destruction and shut out from the presence of the
> Lord and from the majesty of his power on the day he comes
> to be glorified in his holy people and to be marvelled at
> among all those who have believed (2 Thess 1:8–10).

This scripture beautifully summarises both the good news
and the bad news. Those who do not have a relationship
with the Father, made possible only through faith in Jesus
Christ, will be punished with an everlasting destruction.
That everlasting destruction is the lake of fire.

However, it also clearly says that they will be 'shut out
from the presence of the Lord'. How can we now say that
they will also be in his presence? Surely this proves that
the lake of fire cannot be the Holy Spirit?

The word here for 'presence' is the Greek word *proso-
pon*, which means 'face'. That is, the unbelievers will be
shut out from the face of the Lord. In Scripture, the
expression suggests 'to be shut out from fellowship with
God'. *Separation is not a wrong location, but a wrong
relationship*. That is what the unbelievers will not enjoy.

Notice also that the same scripture above says that the
unbelievers will be shut out from the majesty of his power.
It doesn't say that they will be shut out from his power.
They will be feeling the full blast-furnace of it, but there
will be no majesty for them, only torment.

Now let us turn to one of the most interesting scriptures
in the whole Bible. When I saw and understood this, I
realised that all we have been discussing must be true. The
last piece of the jigsaw puzzle fell into perfect place.

In Revelation 14, the prophecy is warning anyone who

worships the beast and receives his mark, that 'he, too, will drink of the wine of God's fury, which has been poured full strength into the cup of his wrath. He will be tormented with burning sulphur *in the presence of the holy angels and of the Lamb*. And the smoke of their torment rises for ever and ever' (Rev 14:10–11, my emphasis). This is obviously referring to destruction in the lake of fire, since the smoke goes up for ever and ever. And this torment takes place *in the presence of the Lord*. Therefore God is there after all! However, as I imagine you have already guessed, the Greek word used here for presence is a different one from the previous example. Here the word is *enopion* and has more the meaning of 'in the sight of', meaning, if you like, 'while he stood by'. This presence is different. It implies that God is there, but that there is no fellowship. In the same way that spectators at a football match are there but do not enjoy the company of the players, so God is present in the lake of fire, but for those who are being eternally destroyed there, there is no fellowship.

Outside the city

The third main objection to the lake of fire being the consuming fire of God's presence is that it is described as being outside the holy city, the New Jerusalem, in the same way that the Valley of Hinnom is outside the Jerusalem of today. For example, in Revelation 22:15 we read that 'outside' are all the unrighteous—the same ones who are described in Revelation 21:8 as those whose place is in the lake of fire. So therefore the lake of fire is outside the city. This is surely symbolic of a different place, away from the existence of God.

But there is a common misconception about the New Jerusalem. Many think that it is describing heaven, but it

is not. In his vision, John says that one of the seven angels
came and said to him: "Come, I will show you the bride,
the wife of the Lamb." And he carried me away in the
Spirit to a mountain great and high, and showed me the
Holy City, Jerusalem, coming down out of heaven from
God' (Rev 21:9–10).

So the Holy City of Revelation is the bride, not heaven.
Now the bride of Christ is his church, and his church is
made up of all those who will be with him, enjoying his
fellowship for ever and ever. So the heavenly city which is
described in such detail is not how heaven will be, but
how the church will be. We learn more of this in the final
chapter. But now we see that it makes sense to say that the
unbelievers and unrighteous 'dogs' will be outside,
because there is no place for them in the church; that is,
enjoying the fellowship of God. That fellowship with God
is heaven, a result of our being declared righteous in his
sight, by his grace, through faith in the saving power of
Jesus Christ.

As we have seen therefore throughout this book, our
reaction to God doesn't depend upon him, for he is
constant, faithful, unchanging, the same yesterday, today
and for ever. And holy. Our reaction to God depends upon
us and our spiritual state. It is that which affects our
relationship with God in our lifetime, and why should
we think that it will be any different after our death?

Therefore the lake of fire is indeed the Holy Fire. But it
is a very different manifestation of the Holy Spirit from
when he comes upon the believer. Here we see the full
strength of the cup of his wrath, reacting inevitably,
eternally and in violent destruction upon those who have
spat at his glory by refusing to believe in him and his
Christ.

Here is the reason for us to understand how dangerous
and futile it is to reject his warnings, given to us through

the Bible, through the prophets and throughout history. God is a consuming fire. We had better make sure we are right before God, otherwise his presence will consume us for ever. We will all spend an eternity in his presence, but how is that eternity to be?

In an African country long ago there was a wise old man who travelled from village to village giving advice and counsel. He always gave good answers to the people's problems and was greatly esteemed. But there was a small boy who was irritated by the old man's eternal wisdom. 'I shall prove him wrong at least once,' he said to himself, and set about thinking how he was to do it. At last he found a solution. 'I shall catch a butterfly,' he thought, 'and I shall hold it alive in my closed hand. I shall go to the old man and ask him, ''Dead or alive?'' If he says, ''Alive,'' I shall crush it secretly in my hand, and show him the dead butterfly. If he says, ''Dead,'' I shall release it to fly away, and all the village will see that he is not infallible.'

The day came when the old man returned, and the little boy ran to him with a closed hand. 'Dead or alive?' he cried. The old sage looked at the hand and at the boy. After a long silence he replied, 'That depends upon you.'

If we deliberately keep on sinning after we have received the knowledge of the truth, no sacrifice for sins is left, but only a fearful expectation of judgment and of raging fire that will consume the enemies of God. . . . It is a dreadful thing to fall into the hands of the living God (Heb 10:26–27, 31).

11

Glorious Fire

Raw power is awesome. I remember the first time I stood on the banks of Niagara Falls. I was awestruck by the sheer power of the earth-shaking wall of water that seemed to roll in slow motion over the edge, crashing into the spume far below. I sensed a gut-wrenching emotion akin to fear. Something much more fundamental than the majesty of the water moved my soul. I became aware of the Somebody behind it, and suddenly the waterfall was no more than an atom in the cosmos. I had had a glimpse of glory.

In the face of the full-force fire of God's glory, we are totally overcome. Those who come close, we read in the Bible, fall face down 'helpless' or 'as though dead'. It is a measure of our continuing need of purification that we are, in this world, unable to stand up to the blaze of such glory. And it is a measure of his perfection that Jesus glowed with the same fire on the Mount of Transfiguration, and now sits at the right hand of the Father in that same glory.

That God is a consuming fire has been a constant theme of this book. But he isn't really! If there was no sin, no potential pollutant to the all-consuming purity of God, then there would be no consuming fire, for there would be nothing to consume. God in himself consumes nothing or no one, but rather glorifies them. He is ultimately a God of glory, whose glory shines 'brighter than the noonday sun'. It is only when the unholy approaches that glory that the fireworks happen, as we have seen. But it was not just because Jesus was sinless that he glowed.

The brief encounter the disciples had with the shining Jesus on the mountain was a glimpse of the real Jesus; a small chink in the wall. Until then his glory had been largely veiled, the disciples only able to guess vaguely at his true nature. They had seen a man, but believed by faith that he was much more. They had seen the miracles, the healings, the casting out of demons; they had seen the wind and waves obey him, and they had believed. But they still had no idea of the unlimited power hidden behind the veil of his human flesh.

No fire without smoke

For now we 'see through a glass, darkly' (1 Cor 13:12, KJV), and God does this deliberately for our own protection. The Jews well understood that to see God was to be consumed, for God himself states in Exodus 33:20, 'You cannot see my face . . . and live.' So when such glory manifests on earth it often takes the form of fire, for that is the most powerful consuming force that exists in nature. After all, the sun is only a fireball, and God is far more glorious and powerful than the sun. Even if God manifested his glory to us as the sun, he would have 'toned down' his majesty a billion-fold in order for us to be able to comprehend it, and even then we would be instantly fried. The power of him who made the galaxies out of his glory is beyond our imagining.

God therefore will not allow anyone too close to his face. He loves us too much. Moses asked to see God's glory, and was told: 'When my glory passes by, I will put you in a cleft in the rock and cover you with my hand until I have passed by. Then I will remove my hand and you will see my back; but my face must not be seen' (Exod 33:22–23). Even Moses—who was the most humble man on earth, and one to whom God had spoken as friend to friend and told him that he was pleased with him and knew him by name—even he couldn't look upon the full light of God's glory which shines from his face.

So it is that whenever God manifests his glory to man, instead of pure fire we see softened fire so that we are not destroyed. Often God uses smoke, or mist, or a cloud, to soften the light of his glory. Before long, the Israelites had learned that the cloud signified God's glorious presence. Sometimes, such as when Solomon dedicated the temple, the cloud of glory was so full of power that the Levites were unable to continue their ministry. At other times the mist was not much more than a shadow in the sunlight. Many people today have seen that cloud and have been awed by God's majesty. Jack Hayford describes such a scene, for example, when he saw his church filled with a glowing mist which had no natural explanation.[1] God himself confirmed to him what he was seeing—the glory of God. But God's face we do not see.

Fire to share

Some, therefore, have concluded that God is hiding his face because he jealously guards his glory. Quoting Isaiah 42 and 48, they insist that God keeps his glory for himself alone: 'I am the Lord; that is my name! I will not give my glory to another or my praise to idols' (Is 42:8); and: 'For my own sake, for my own sake, I do this. How can I let myself be defamed? I will not yield my glory to another' (Is 48:11).

As Jack Hayford explains, 'Isaiah's prophecy did and does emphasize God's refusal to share His glory with another.'[2] But we need to know what or who 'another' is, and he rightly concludes that the context of both scriptures shows that God is referring to idols and demons. God certainly has no intention of letting the devil steal one flicker of his glory. But he is not referring to man, less still his precious adopted sons in Christ. With us he wants to share his glory. In fact, it is his express intention to do so from the beginning of time. How could the Maker of all things, themselves such a reflection and declaration of his glory (Ps 19:1), *not* want to share it?

Paul reminds us: 'All have sinned and fall short of the glory of God' (Rom 3:23). From this we see that it is in sinning that we fall short of God's glory, so when the sin is removed by the blood of Christ, that glory is restored. Restoration to righteousness *must* be accompanied by a restoration of glory. That is God's purpose. Therefore the sons of God, those reconciled through the cleansing blood of Christ, must share in his glory. The Bible is full of such references:[3] 'Now if we are children, then we are heirs—heirs of God and co-heirs with Christ, if indeed we share in his sufferings in order *that we may also share in his glory*' (Rom 8:17, my emphasis).

And 2 Thessalonians 2:14 says, 'He called you to this through our gospel, that *you might share in the glory* of our Lord Jesus Christ.' Again my emphasis shows that we are to *share* in his glory. This is what we are called for. Glory is our inheritance.

This glory is both for eternity and for today. During the Lord's Gethsemane prayer recorded in John 17, Jesus points out to the Father that he has already shared his glory with his disciples when he says, 'I have given them the glory that you gave me, that they may be one as we are one' (Jn 17:22). So it is for today.

If we already have some of God's glory, what is this glory, and how do we perceive it? It is evident that we do not all go around with faces shining like that of Moses

when he came down from the mountain after his encounter
there with God. At that time he had to put a veil over his
face so that the Israelites could look at him. Churches
today are not filled with veiled believers lighting up the
sanctuaries with their holy glow (yet)!

Our glory on earth

Actually there is no reason why such manifestations
shouldn't occur. God can show us his glory whenever
and however he wants. A year or two ago, in the city of
Porto Alegre, Brazil, a young man took a photo of his
church's youth meeting. The teenagers were singing and
worshipping God. When the film was developed, the feet
and legs of the youngsters were clearly visible, but their
upper bodies were totally engulfed in what looked like
flames. The camera and film were professionally checked,
and the other photos on the film were perfectly normal.
There were no abnormalities, except this one photo. Each
individual seemed to be a flaming torch! It seems that, like
Elisha's servant who saw the chariots of fire in 2 Kings 6,
we may occasionally see the fire of God revealed.

The character of Christ

But we agree this is not God's usual method of witness to
his glory through the church. We have seen that Holy Fire
destroys the unholy but edifies and glorifies the holy.
Therefore the believer can expect to manifest this fire.
How is it normally seen then? John tells us: 'The Word
was made flesh, and dwelt among us, (and we beheld his
glory, the glory as of the only begotten of the Father,) full
of grace and truth' (Jn 1:14, KJV).

Jesus is the glory of the Father; indeed he is the
'radiance of God's glory' (Heb 1:3), which means that if

we see Jesus we see the glory of God. Therefore we manifest the glory of God when we are as Jesus is. So the first way that we reflect his glory is through our character.

Man, according to 1 Corinthians 11:7, 'is the image and glory of God'. The two concepts are inextricably linked. It is the image or likeness which brings the glory. The word for 'glory' is in the Hebrew *chabod*, which means 'the weight, value or worth of a person or thing'. Someone of great social standing makes a strong impression upon those around him; that is, he is of great weight. If the Queen of England were to walk into a cocktail party, I guarantee that every conversation would change. In the worldly sense, that is glory. If her attendant walked into the same party, someone whom nobody knew or had even heard of, she would be treated with almost equal deference. That is reflected glory.

In the book of Esther, the evil Haman attempted to take such reflected glory for himself, but through Esther's intervention King Xerxes forced Haman to give the honours instead to Mordecai the Jew. Then Haman robed Mordecai, and led him on horseback through the city streets, proclaiming before him, 'This is what is done for the man the king delights to honour!' (Esther 6:11). Like light, reflected glory is no less glory because it is reflected. It is real enough.

The *chabod* of God is his weight. If something heavy rests upon something soft, the soft thing takes up the impression or seal of the weighty object. If it is then removed, an imprint is left there which reflects the heavy object; how accurately depends upon how pliable the softer object is.

Like a seal pressed into sealing wax is the glory of God into our lives, and we can thus reflect his glory if we will be moulded into his likeness. So it is that the Holy Spirit is referred to as our seal, guaranteeing our inheritance. He is the weight of God's glory impressing our lives, changing our character to his. Sealing wax must be heated to take the seal, to soften it, and in the same way we must expect to go through challenges and trials in order to soften our hearts so that we might better reflect his character: 'And we, who with unveiled faces all reflect the Lord's glory, are being transformed into his likeness with ever-increasing glory, which comes from the Lord, who is the Spirit' (2 Cor 3:18).

If our faces are unveiled, we will reveal the character of Christ. If the veil of our soul obscures the light with impurity, the reflection dims. It is said that before the age of thirty we inherit our face, but after that age we have earned it! The older we get, the more our face reflects our character. A sour person has a down-turned mouth. A happy person has smile wrinkles. In the same way our character reflects the glory of God. A dirty mirror blurs the image. In a freshly cleaned one, the face is clear, revealing the full character.

The Bible speaks of the glory of man: 'All men are like grass, and all their glory is like the flowers of the field. The grass withers and the flowers fall, because the breath of the Lord blows on them. Surely the people are grass. The grass withers and the flowers fall, but the word of our God stands for ever' (Is 40:6–8).

Man's glory is made up of temporal things that fade—our beauty, our intelligence, our strength. But as John the Baptist said, 'He must become greater; I must become less' (Jn 3:30). As the fire of the Holy Spirit blows upon us, the glory of man must fade and give way to the surpassing glory, which is the glory of God, which will never fade or pass away, but rather it will grow.

For this glory which we are reflecting is an ever-increasing glory. This can only mean that the process has already begun, and will continue for ever! Therefore the glory we receive from the Lord is not just reserved for eternity, as though we must wait until we are with God in heaven before we are given any. Certainly there will be surpassing glory there, but we have already begun on the road of glory. Then we shall be shining like a comet; for now, we are just 'trailing wisps of glory'.

Conversion

Christlikeness *is* the glory of God. This is probably the first evidence the world sees of the power of God at work. When violent street gang leaders of the inner city become gentle giants of faith, there is no greater testimony to the all-changing power of the glory of God. The pages of the Lamb's book of life are filled with prostitutes and drunkards whose lives have been turned around to become glorious examples of grace and truth. Such is the love of God. Such power brings glory to the only One who could do such a thing. So this ability of God to change character brings glory to the process of doing so. Paul asks: 'Will not the ministry of the Spirit be even more glorious? If the ministry that condemns men is glorious, how much more glorious is the ministry that brings righteousness!' (2 Cor 3:8–9).

The ministry of preaching the gospel and seeing the lost won is perhaps the greatest single manifestation of the glory of God. Nothing replaces it. Nothing exceeds it.

Miracles

But such a ministry doesn't stop at that, marvellous though it is. The church also manifests the glory of God when, by faith, we take hold of God's power within us to work miracles. Jesus, encouraged by his mother, solved a ticklish problem for his host at the wedding at Cana by turning water into wine and 'thus revealed his glory, and his disciples put their faith in him' (Jn 2:11).

Miracles may be counterfeited, but cannot be discounted. There are simply too many millions who can testify to having been miraculously healed. Let me add one more. It is a small thing, but I know what happened and can verify it to be true. I myself suffered for many years from verrucae on my right foot. I had had them treated to no avail; in fact they had grown even larger. One morning in Buenos Aires I was washing my foot in the shower and discovered that they were not there. They had been there the day before as large as life, but now they had simply gone! I blinked, and checked my foot. There was not even a scar. (Feeling foolish, I even checked my other foot. That's how surprised I was!) Nothing. Then I remembered that the previous night I had been in a crusade meeting of the evangelist Carlos Anacondia, and there had been a prayer for the sick. At that time I hadn't even thought of such an insignificant thing, but God surely had. Now I know that verrucae can come and go, but they don't naturally do it overnight.

Miracles bring glory to God. Since that time I have personally witnessed hundreds, and the name of the Lord is continuously lifted up through his power at work. God is not glorified by the scoffers and doubters; nor by the charlatan 'healers' either. We have no need to fake healing on God's behalf—he is perfectly capable of managing on his own. But it is wonderful to see genuine miracles, and there is reflected glory in praying for the sick and watching God touch them.

Glorious destruction

The reason the Son of God appeared was to destroy the devil's work (1 Jn 3:8).

Christ came to bring down the kingdom of darkness. The church ministers this victory of Jesus, and it is her glory to do so. Psalm 149 declares that it is 'the glory of the saints' to carry out the sentence written against the nations, peoples, kings and nobles opposed to God; against the powers of darkness. There is glory in destruction of God's enemies.

In Exodus 14:4, God said that he would gain glory for himself through Pharaoh and all his army when they were destroyed in the Red Sea. Again, Ezekiel prophesies: 'This is what the Sovereign Lord says: "I am against you, O Sidon, and I will gain glory within you. They will know that I am the Lord, when I inflict punishment on her and show myself holy within her" ' (Ezek 28:22). Here is forecast the destruction of Sidon which will bring glory to God. By destroying the unholy, God is demonstrating his righteousness and his inability to suffer evil. So his righteous holiness is emphasised. In the same way fire doesn't just consume what it burns, but uses it as fuel which makes the fire hotter.

Today God is glorified whenever prayer or ministry leads to the downfall of Satan's works. Demons are cast out, madmen are restored to their right minds, just like the madman of Gadarene. Recently, a Hindu temple in India closed following the intense prayer of a group of Christians. This led to the salvation of the Hindu priests and the temple prostitute, who was also delivered of many demons. Such victories bring glory to God, and to the church. This is the glory of the saints.

The ultimate victory is the victory over death. In the story of the raising of Lazarus, Jesus tells us that Lazarus died in order that God's Son may be glorified through it (Jn 11:4). Had we been present at the death I think we would have seriously questioned Jesus' love, his motives and his abilities. How could he allow him to die? Couldn't

he see his suffering and that of his sisters? Didn't he say
he loved them? What kind of love is this? Therefore we
would have been without faith, which is why Jesus said to
his disciples, 'For your sake I am glad I was not there, so
that you may believe' (Jn 11:15) and in verse 40 to
Martha, 'Did I not tell you that if you believed, you
would see the glory of God?' And with a mighty shout
the four-day-dead Lazarus came out of the tomb, to the
glory of God!

Faith, glory and anointing

We see according to our faith. Those without faith see
nothing in the spirit, for their eyes are blinded by the god
of this age, but as our faith grows, so we see more. The
veil thins. The cloud of his presence reveals more and
more of his fire which shines through. And as the fire
shines and we see more of his awesome power, our faith
increases—the one working on the other. And as our faith
increases, so does the revealed glory. *Faith is fuel for
glory, and glory burns brighter upon it.*

The measure of the revelation of God's glory in our
lives is called 'anointing'. How much shines through the
veil of our soul? This anointing comes not by the earn-
estness of our desire, nor by the length of our prayers, nor
by our sacrificial efforts 'for the Lord', nor even by
leading a perfectly moral life—though all are good. There
are many from other walks of life and other religions who
are doing these things and see no glory. In Romans 12,
Paul points out that we should use our gifts, not in
accordance with these things, but in accordance with our
faith.

Our anointing comes by faith. It is the trigger which
releases the manifestation of the presence. This is why so
many seemingly 'unfit' people move with such an evident

power of God, such glory in their lives. 'How can that stuck up boaster see so many miracles in his ministry?' we ask. Because he has faith. Of course, we long for the boasting to cease, but the Holy Spirit can bring that about far better than our criticisms can. Thank God that he doesn't wait until we are all perfect before a glint of his glory is released!

However, we need to remember that the manifestation of God's glory cannot be manipulated. God is a sovereign God, and the wind blows where he wills. When God reveals himself in fire, he comes at his own time and in his own way. Of course, he chooses the right moments, such as occasions of worship, commissioning or dedication, but God doesn't respond to a formula: 'We just do this, this and this, and here comes the glory!' Not at all. Every time Jesus healed someone he used a different method precisely so that we would realise that there is no method. There is only grace.

God desires a glorious, radiant church; a beautiful bride for Christ. 'To him be glory in the church and in Christ Jesus throughout all generations, for ever and ever!' states Paul in Ephesians 3:21. We do not strive to take glory for ourselves, because to do so diminishes the glory of God. But we do accept that beautiful reflected glory, and praise him for it. Glory is like everything else in the kingdom of God—the more you give, the more you receive. If we give glory to God, he will glorify his church. Our attitude should be that of Christ Jesus who said: 'I am not seeking glory for myself; but there is one who seeks it, and he is the judge' (Jn 8:50)

Eternal glory

All of the manifestations of the glory on earth are but tiny sparks from the Holy Fire of God. Now we see through a glass darkly, but then we shall see face to face (1 Cor 13:12).

These minuscule revelations have been called by some the *shekinah* glory of God. Judson Cornwall points out that in fact the term means 'the divine presence' or 'divine manifestation' of God, not referring specifically to fire or clouds.[4] It isn't a biblical word, but is used in the Jewish commentaries on the Old Testament. The sense is of *dwelling with*; the glory being inseparable from the presence of God. It is the same thing.

When Jesus comes, he will come on the clouds with great glory. His full glory will be revealed at last. No one will need to guess any longer. That glory will be a consuming fire to all who have denied him, but wonderful majesty to those who await his return with longing. 'For the earth will be filled with the knowledge of the glory of the Lord, as the waters cover the sea' (Hab 2:14). Everyone will know. There will be no arguments. Those who teach that he has already returned have no concept whatsoever of his glory. When he comes it will be like a spiritual nuclear explosion covering the whole earth at once—except that for the unrighteous, the fire will be longer and hotter! We, his church, will be totally swamped in the awe and majesty of the moment.

Heaven is called 'glory'. 'You guide me with your counsel, and afterwards you will take me into glory' (Ps 73:24) is the cry of Asaph, and is our final destiny. At the end of all things, to partake of this ever-increasing glory is the inheritance of the saints. We will share in an eternal glory which has not yet been seen: 'To the elders among you, I appeal as a fellow-elder, a witness of Christ's sufferings and one who also will share in the glory *to be revealed*' (1 Pet 5:1, my emphasis).

The glory of God there will be beyond our imagining. Even in the heaven seen in John's vision it was for a while too great for anyone to enter the temple (Rev 15:8). So it will be.

Our welcome too is beyond understanding. Stephen looked into heaven and saw the glory of God, and Jesus standing at the right hand of God. 'Look,' he said, 'I see heaven open and the Son of Man standing at the right hand of God' (Acts 7:56). But we know that Jesus *sat down* at the right hand of the Father. So here we see him rising to his feet, the Lord himself giving a standing ovation to Stephen, the first to lay down his life for his Saviour. What a mighty reception! And then he doesn't sit back down alone, but with us at his side: 'To him who overcomes, I will give the right to sit with me on my throne, just as I overcame and sat down with my Father on his throne' (Rev 3:21). What unimaginable honour, and what perfect love. *That* is glory.

Shadrach, Meshach and Abednego emerged from the fiery furnace to discover that their whole lives had changed. They had been persecuted and punished for being faithful to God. Now they were being exalted for the same thing. They had gone into the furnace with nothing more than faith, and had emerged with glory. They 'loved not their lives unto the death' and emerged with victory. They had had an encounter with the Holy Fire.

Such glory is only for those redeemed by the precious blood of Jesus. The guilty respond to the Holy Fire in a wholly different way, for the Holy Fire destroys the unrighteous. Holy Fire separates the holy from the unholy and consumes sin. Holy Fire is eternal fire, and will consume the unrighteous for ever. Let us be certain that each one of us knows how we shall respond to the Holy Fire when he comes. Come, Holy Fire!

Notes

1. Jack Hayford, *Glory on Your House* (Kingsway, 1992), pp. 13–16.
2. *Ibid*, p. 20.
3. For example, see also Psalm 3:3; Isaiah 60:1–3; 62:1–3; Luke 2:32; Romans 2:10; 9:23; 1 Corinthians 11:7; 1 Thessalonians 2:12; 1 Peter 4:14.
4. Judson Cornwall, *Meeting God* (Creation House, 1987).

Christ for all Nations

Christ for all Nations was established in 1974 in South Africa, by German evangelist Reinhard Bonnke. After working as a missionary in Lesotho for seven years, God gave him a recurring dream of Africa being washed in the blood of Jesus, and the Holy Spirit spoke to him saying, 'Africa shall be saved.'

From that moment, Reinhard Bonnke dedicated his life to the task of taking the gospel from Cape Town to Cairo. It began as a tent ministry, first with a 10,000-seater tent, then a 35,000-seater—the largest mobile structure in the world.

In 1986 Reinhard held what would be the first of many Fire Conferences in Harare, Zimbabwe, during which it was prophesied that God would multiply the anointing upon his ministry. From that day the crowds grew dramatically and soon the tent was too small. By 1990 the crowds were topping the half-million mark.

During this period the headquarters of the mission moved to Frankfurt, Germany, where they are today. The vision remains strong for Africa, and Reinhard Bonnke still preaches there regularly, but more recently other nations have been visited, and the crusade ministry is now international.

In 1993 Reinhard Bonnke heard the Lord leading him to place an evangelistic booklet in every home in the British Isles, and in April 1994 nearly 25 million booklets were delivered. In September 1995 this ambitious project was repeated in Germany, Austria and Switzerland. Future plans for further booklet drops include the United States and Canada.

Further details of Pastor Bonnke and the work of the mission can be obtained from Christ for all Nations, Missionszentrale, Postfach 60 05 74, D-6000 Frankfurt 60, Germany; or in the UK from Highway House, 250 Coombs Road, Halesowen, West Midlands B62 8AA, UK.

Evangelism by Fire

by Reinhard Bonnke

The evangelist Reinhard Bonnke has seen up to two million men and women pressing forward for salvation in a single year. Miracles of healing take place constantly.

That is in Africa – but why not in the West also? *Evangelism by Fire* explores the same exciting possibilities for every continent and nation.

If you are tired of simply talking about evangelism, and now ready for action, then let this book introduce you to a new dimension of Spirit-led evangelism.

'*Evangelism by Fire* helps us understand some of the spiritual dynamics underlying this phenomenal charismatic movement. At the present time Bonnke may possibly be distinguished as the Christian evangelist heard live and in person by more individuals month in and month out than any other.' – Dr C. PETER WAGNER
Professor of Church Growth,
Fuller Theological Seminary, USA

REINHARD BONNKE is the founder and leader of 'Christ for all Nations', an international evangelistic ministry with headquarters in Frankfurt, Germany. With a burning passion for the lost and a desire to see church leaders inspired to Holy Spirit evangelism, he has conducted gospel campaigns and 'Fire' conferences throughout Africa and the rest of the world. Signs and wonders follow the preaching of the gospel, with crowds of up to half a million people gathered in a single service.

 Kingsway Publications

Mighty Manifestations

by Reinhard Bonnke

The Holy Spirit manifests His power in the lives of men and women of God so that they may do what He wants done.

So why is it that these 'manifestations' – tongues, prophecy, healing and supernatural knowledge – are so often the cause of controversy and confusion?

Reinhard Bonnke is perhaps more qualified than most to shed light on what it means to minister in the power of the Spirit, having personally done so to literally millions of people in many parts of the world. Here he offers a 'back to the Bible' examination of the spiritual gifts listed in 1 Corinthians 12. These are not given so that we may congratulate ourselves, or polish up our church's image, but to endorse the preaching of the Gospel to those around us.

A book not only to increase our understanding, but to energise us for action.

'One reason why God's blessing will be upon this book is because this man of God keeps things in perspective: the Cross and Christ are always pre-eminent, his love for people predominant, his teaching always to bless people and glorify God.'

– COLIN WHITTAKER
Editor, Redemption Magazine, UK

Kingsway Publications